Teacher-to-Teacher Series

D1365967

NEA Teacher-to-Teacher Books

Printing History
First Printing: March 1994

NOTE: The opinions expressed in this book should not be construed as representing the policy or position of the National Education Association. Materials published by the NEA Professional Library are intended to be discussion documents for educators who are concerned with specialized interests of the profession.

CREDITS: *Editor:* Mary Dalheim. *Production Coordinator:* Linda Brunson. *Art Design:* NoBul Graphics.

Library of Congress Cataloging-in-Publication Data
Time strategies.
      p. cm. — (Teacher to teacher series)
  Includes bibliographical references.
  ISBN 0-8106-2902-X
    1. Teachers — United States — Time management. 2. School management and organization — United States. 3. Educational change — United States.
I.Series.
LB2838.8.T56 1994
371.1' 02 —dc20   ◄████► 20   93-47488
                        CIP

Contents

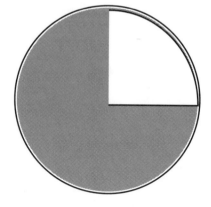

How to Use this Book

Time Strategies is no ordinary book. It is part of the NEA Professional Library's Teacher-to-Teacher series in which classroom teachers speak directly to other teachers—like you—about their school restructuring efforts.

Printed in the upper right-hand corner of every book cover in the series is a routing slip that encourages you to pass the book on to colleagues once you have read it—in other words, to spread the word about school change.

Book topics cover areas such as large-scale school change, student assessment, cross-age grouping, and integrating students with special needs into regular classrooms.

Read the Five Stories

Inside each book you will find stories from five or more teachers across the country who discuss, step by step, how they tackled a specific restructuring challenge. They will describe what worked and didn't work, and provide you with any diagrams, checklists, or tables they think other teachers would find useful.

Write Your Own Ideas in this Book

At the end of each story in a book is an area called Reader Reflec-tions. This area is for you and any colleague who reads the story to write related insights and action points for your school or school district to consider.

You see, the purpose of the Teacher-to-Teacher series is not only to spread the word about school change, but to encourage other teachers to partici-pate in its exploration.

Discuss Your Thoughts With Others

Once you have routed a book through your school, you can meet with colleagues who contributed to the Read-er Reflections sections and expand upon your thoughts.

Go Online

Believe it or not, the communication and sharing doesn't have to stop there. If you would like to discuss a Teacher-to-Teacher book series topic with teach-ers across the country, you can. Any NEA mem-ber who subscribes to the America Online electronic network can participate in an ongo-ing forum on these book topics.

The National Educa-tion Association's area on the network is called NEA Online. Once signed on to NEA On-line, just keyword to *NEA Prof Library*.

To subscribe to NEA Online, call 1-800-827-6364, ext. 8544.

Introduction

TIMELOCK: When demands on our time become so overwhelming that it feels impossible to wring one more second out of crowded schedules and hectic days.

(Keyes, 1992)

Just about every teacher in America knows about timelock. That's because most school schedules do not afford teachers the time they need to meet the mounting demands of classroom teaching, to engage in professional development activities, to work with one another, to participate in community forums — and — to restructure school operations. One of the most challenging elements in any school improvement project, is determining what can be done with the use of time in schools so that teachers can do all the teaching, learning, collaborating, communicating, and restructuring that they need to do.

Escaping the Tyranny of Time

The special time report, the five stories, and the 12 short stories that appear in *Time Strategies* investigate this time dilemma and the ways educators are finding to unlock the bonds of time. For example:

• In Florida, the Pinellas Classroom Teachers Association and its local district administrators developed a number of approaches to handling time that have freed up teachers to work on school restructuring projects. In this book, you'll read how Pinellas educators managed to earmark supplemental funds to pay for substitutes for two professional release days per teacher, how they adopted four Early Release days that provide a total of 12 additional hours for teacher collaboration, and how they made faculty meetings more time efficient.

• You'll discover how the faculty at Wasson High School in Colorado Springs, Colorado, developed a block scheduling plan in which students attend four 90-minute instructional periods instead of their traditional seven 50-minute periods. The longer periods allow more in-depth study, individualization, and interdisciplinary tie-ins for the students, and they give all teachers a full 90-minute planning period each day to be used for collaboration and curriculum development.

• Teachers from two other schools, Travis High School in Austin, Texas, and Parkland High School in Winston-Salem, North Carolina, admired the Wasson Block Schedule so much that they adapted the plan to suit their students' specific needs. In *Time Strategies*, teachers from both schools tell how they made the block schedule "their own" as well as how they solicited administrative and community support to do so.

• When curriculum changes drove teachers at North Eugene High School to restructure their school day,

they predicted the change would take some getting used to. In the fifth story in this book, three North Eugene staffers tell how teachers collaborated to ensure a smooth and timely transition.

• A final section in *Time Strategies*, entitled Short Stories, briefly describes how 11 other elementary, middle, and high schools across the country have devised strategies to combat timelock. These include: (1) structuring "schools within a school" groupings of students and teachers to provide more flexible sharing of resource teachers, (2) enlisting students, teachers, and administrators to cover teachers' classes, and (3) scheduling days into the calendar year for teacher planning.

Strategies Are Not Enough

As the stories in *Time Strategies* reveal, there are many strategies for freeing up, buying, and restructuring time that can ease the pressure imposed on teachers. But such strategies are not enough.

I think every storyteller in this book will agree that the way to permanently release teachers from the bonds of timelock is to officially redefine their role in a way that automatically builds in more time for learning, collaborating, communicating, and restructuring. In today's schools these activities are frequently dismissed as "noninstructional duties" that are not central to the teaching and learning process. That

perception must change.

As Susan Moore Johnson says in *Teachers at Work*:

A lone teacher can impart phonics, fractions, the pluperfect tense, or the periodic table, but only through teachers' collective efforts will schools produce educated graduates who can read and compute, apply scientific principles, comprehend the lesson of history, value others' cultures and speak their languages, and conduct themselves responsibly as citizens. Such accomplishments are the product of a corporate venture.

Establishing and maintaining a successful corporate venture requires time. ◆

Mary Dalheim
Series Editor

Additional Considerations for Unlocking Time Constraints

Education researchers suggest you consider the following factors when reconceptualizing school time:

☐ Give attention to both individual and institutional needs (Coalition of Essential Schools, 1991).

☐ Be sensitive to the local context (Jacokes, 1990; Hargreaves, 1990).

☐ Involve all stakeholders in the decision making (Jacokes, 1990).

☐ Foster movement from present-day concerns to long-term concerns (Hargreaves, 1990).

☐ Make every effort to convince policymakers that professional, noninstructional time must be built in to every teacher's job (Coalition for Essential Schools, 1991).

☐ Encourage both faculty members and administrators to use vision, mission, and goals to prioritize and focus the use of time (Center for Organization and Restructuring Schools, 1992).

☐ Strive to decelerate, to accomplish more by doing less, and to accept the discomforting fact that you can't do everything (Keyes, 1992).

Source: *Doubts and Certainties* newsletter, 1992.

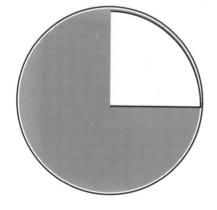

IT'S ABOUT TIME!

A Report from the National Education Association's Special Committee on Time Resources
July, 1993

Across the nation in schools and districts engaged in transforming schools into more effective learning communities, the issue that has emerged as the most intense and the one that universally dominates discussion is time. As educators are working to change schools to better serve students for the twenty-first century, time constraints are posing the most daunting problems. In a recent *Education Week* series, time was identified as one of seven key areas where change must occur for school reform to succeed. In the time segment of this series, Sommerfeld asserts, "We Have Met the Enemy, And They Are Hours." (*Education Week,* 1993)

Educators are besieged by a multiplicity of demands that preclude adequate time for planning, reflecting, collaborating, researching, and assessing. The shortage of time is a problem in all schools and is one of the most complex and challenging problems teachers face every day. These time limitations impact the working lives of teachers and other school employees, causing frustration and inhibiting change.

The primary dilemma is that school personnel require *time* to restructure, *while* restructuring time. Unlike other enterprises that shut down to redesign, retool, and re-inventory, schools must continue to provide effective learning experiences for students without interruption while changes in pedagogy, curriculum, and organization are being constructed, implemented, and assessed. Redesigning schools is not something educators can or should be asked to do in their "spare time." Staff must be provided more development time and greater authority to control the use of that time. Resolution of the time issue remains one of the most critical problems confronting educators today.

The 1992 National Education Association Representative Assembly, cognizant of the impact of the time issue, passed the following new business item:

The National Education Association (NEA) shall establish a committee to address the issue of time resources. The scope shall include but not be limited to the following:

1. The impact of school restructuring and the related time needs of NEA members

2. Strategies to help local and state associations attract members as participants who enhance local and state NEA affiliates

The primary dilemma is that school personnel require time to restructure while restructuring time.

3. Implications for length of school day, school year, release time, compensation, and other related time resource issues.

The Committee's findings and recommendations shall be presented at the 1993 Representative Assembly. (1992-52)

The Time Committee was appointed and began its deliberations early in 1993. The Committee reviewed a vast amount of research and status reports, heard testimony, conducted interviews, and considered several time innovations.

Confronting the Time Dilemma

The Committee feels the following issues, while not totally inclusive, do represent the major time dilemmas faced by teachers and other school employees.

Time Limits

Time is a finite resource; its use must be planned and allocated efficaciously, both for adults in the school system and for students. Time is the basic dimension through which teachers' work is constructed and interpreted. Time often defines the possibilities and limitations of teachers' professional performance.

For the Committee, the difficulty is not how much TIME, but instead, how that resource is used. "Through the prism of time, we ... can begin to see ways in which teachers construct the nature of their work at the same time as they are constrained by it." (Hargreaves, 1990) For school employees involved in reform, time has become an implacable barrier. Existing structures and time frames do not afford the necessary time to work collaboratively; to plan, implement, and evaluate quality programs for children; and to engage in an assortment of professional development activities.

Time as the Driver

Time fuels the system. In traditional, regimented school schedules, time has been the constant and learning the variable. It seems logical to the Committee that the imperative for improving schools is to reverse that dictum — learning must be the constant and time the variable.

By reducing children to a common denominator to support administrative and legislative requirements for counting and sorting, individual student differences and learning patterns are discarded. Too frequently, decisions impacting learning, teaching, and curriculum are based on administrative convenience (e.g., length and number of periods in the

day, school calendars, Carnegie units, testing requirements), rather than on the learning needs of students.

Every professional educator understands the inherent fallacy of requiring each child to spend the same number of hours in school, complete the same number of courses, attend school for the same number of years, fulfill the same standardized test requirements. Proponents of a more student-centered approach believe that schools need more flexible structures, enabling students to take as much or as little time as necessary to master their coursework and providing teachers control over the time required to prepare and teach and evaluate their lessons. Liberating pedagogy and the curriculum from time constraints enhances teaching and learning.

Time for Professional Development

Traditionally, teachers' work has been and continues to be viewed as time spent "in front of the classroom." Such a perception reinforces the concept that teachers are primarily deliverers of content; that curricular planning and decision making are vested at higher levels of authority; that professional development is unrelated to improving instruction. Given this view of teachers' work, it is hardly surprising that teachers experience intense guilt and a feeling of divided loyalties and responsibilities when professional duties take them away from the classroom.

As teachers and other school employees partici-

pate as equal stakeholders (joining parents, students, business/community leaders, policymakers, and others) in the reform process, they are demanding a share in the control of school time and its use. Currently, very little of a

teacher's nominal workday is available for the discretionary use of the professional.

The assumption that teachers and their time use must be "controlled" emanates from the historically low status of teachers and is related to issues of trust and respect. For example, at the turn of the century, a bell-ringing clock-timer device, the Autocrat, was installed in schools to monitor teachers' use of time. (Purnell and Hill, 1992) Teachers

...the single most important resource for effective school improvement is time with colleagues: time to examine, time to debate, time to reflect.

have not been trusted to use their noninstructional time wisely and have had virtually no control over the structure or use of their time. Current research literature supports

that when professionals have authentic opportunities to organize and control their work setting, performance increases. (Firestone and Rosenblum, 1988)

A critical requirement to sustain and support school restructuring is ongoing, meaningful interaction among educators. Too frequently, current professional development activities are restricted to district-mandated workshops, training programs, and inservice experiences delivered by an external authority. These activities, often viewed by professionals as attempts simply to expose them to current educational fads or trends, are frequently considered squandered time. Professional development activities involving staff in collaborative, interactive experiences

represent a more productive allocation of time. "Collaborative work with peers increases teachers' sense of affiliation with the school and their sense of mutual support and responsibility for the effectiveness of instruction." (Little, 1984)

"Such professional development activities must be staff-determined, ongoing, sustained, and supported over time." (Louis and Smith, 1990)

Reports from countries around the globe indicate that the best professional development activity for educators is meaningful dialogue and reflection among colleagues. Unlike the solitary endeavor that characterizes teaching in the United States, Asian pedagogy is approached as a group effort. In Japan and Taiwan, for example, teachers are in charge of

classes only 60 percent of the time they are in school. (Stevenson, 1992) In Beijing, teachers instruct students in the classroom three hours daily; their remaining time is dedicated to interacting with colleagues, planning and assessing, tutoring students, or participating in a variety of professionally enriching activities. Experiences from overseas indicate that when professional development opportunities are a designated and significant part of the teachers' work environment, higher quality learning for students can be achieved. (Price, 1993)

Current research reveals unequivocally that time for collaboration, dialogue, and reflection among professionals is essential. (Center on Organization and Restructuring of Schools, 1992) Discussions with practitioners reaffirm that the single most important and necessary resource for effective school improvement is time with colleagues: time to examine, time to debate, time to reflect.

Working Conditions

School employees' working conditions are also children's learning conditions. Although 10 years have elapsed since *A Nation at Risk* and other reports strongly advocating the need for comprehensive change, the configuration of the school day, the allocation and availability of resources, the number of students assigned to a teacher, the paucity of technology and other updated instructional materials, and the protracted use of aging or woefully inadequate school facilities reflect an outdated, autocratic system.

The control school employees have over their working environment has changed little and in some cases has diminished. Despite volumes of research data and a chorus of practitioners shouting to be heard and empowered, working conditions and increased opportunities for professionals remain largely mired in the status quo.

School employees' working conditions and students' learning conditions are inextricably intertwined. In a recent study, Louis comments, "Concentrated time and effort must be directed to maximizing effective teacher development in order to realize student empowerment and to increase student achievement." It is impossible to change learning conditions for students if we do not change the working conditions of school employees. (Louis and Smith, 1990)

Time for School Reform

The reform movement itself is imposing time constraints that are impacting school personnel. In many places, reform efforts have simply been added to the list of priorities school employees are expected to perform daily. Time must be stretched further to accommodate staff participation in governance issues, curriculum development, action research, student assessment, program evaluation, and community involvement activities.

"If the recent reforms are to succeed, students and teachers must not simply absorb a new body of knowledge. Rather, they must acquire a new way of thinking about knowledge and a new practice of acquiring it." (Price, 1993) Teachers and other school employees must now learn new information, new process skills, new strategies for new instructional efforts (e.g., team teaching, cross-age learning, interdisciplinary instruction, peer coaching, cooperative learning, and/or whole language). These contemporary teaching skills necessitate teacher interaction and collaboration to produce reform; consequently, more time must be devoted for professional development activities in order to achieve reform efforts than was required in the past.

Rather than ameliorating conditions, school reform is creating one more behemoth responsibility for teachers to embrace. Teaching is an exhausting occupation. With little down time for self-renewal and celebration, educators cannot accept adding time demands to those already imposed on professionals without restructuring time itself. Little wonder that frustration and burnout are common companions with many school reform activities.

Time and the Increasing Needs of Students

Profound changes that are occurring in society, the home environment, and the workplace have invaded schools, increasing exponentially the number and types of interactions teachers must conduct with children on a daily basis. The time burden looms large as schools are forced to extend their custodial responsibilities for children to include performing social services previously assigned to human services agencies as well as confronting the myriad problems concerning health, safety, and well-being inherent in today's very needy school populations. These time demands must be factored in with the increased time pressures teachers face as they address the burgeoning amount of knowledge and skills today's students are required to master.

Additionally, most teachers are realizing new demands on their time as special needs children are being mainstreamed into classrooms in a sincere effort to improve their academic performance and socialization skills. In many cases, the support provided to those teachers is inadequate or nonexistent.

An important requisite for quality integrated education for special needs students is comprehensive personnel development for all education employees to acquire the specific skills, knowledge, and resources necessary for teaching students with diverse learning problems and highly specific physical needs. Coordinated planning time is required for special educators to work with their colleagues to design and implement individualized programs that best serve the needs of these students. Teachers cannot do it alone. While the goals are meritorious, each special needs child places additional time demands on school personnel.

Seeking Immediate Relief

The Committee believes that addressing the problem of time constraints requires long-term solutions. The final section of this report offers several specific recommendations designed to resolve the complex time concerns that confront school personnel. However, the Committee contends that immediate relief is also necessary to ameliorate current time problems. The Committee sets forth several suggestions designed to help professional educators provide short-term relief to their time crisis. The majority of the suggestions below were culled from experiences in the National Education Association's school renewal projects and from selected experiences of other schools and school districts. Additional information detailing these strategies may be obtained from the NEA's Center for Teaching and Learning.

Five time dilemma strategies emerged from the work being conducted in these innovative sites. These strategies are not mutually exclusive; they represent five different ways educators facing time dilemmas have attempted to assuage the acute problem of finding time.

Time Strategy #1: Freed-Up Time

Many schools are freeing teachers' time from traditional constraints. This time strategy does not attempt to restructure the calendar, the school day, or teaching schedules, but rather to break teachers from traditional constraints by various intervention tactics. Generally, these tactics are temporary, ad hoc, and may have cost and contractual implications. Some efforts, however, are being made to institutionalize these efforts.

Various strategies to free teachers from direct student supervision include:
• Enlisting administrators to teach classes
• Authorizing teaching assistants and college interns to teach classes at regular intervals under the direction of a teacher
• Teaming teachers, both formally and informally, allowing one teacher to instruct for another
• Combining classes with a coordinated community event so teachers may collaborate

• Formulating plans for all-day student-planned and teacher-approved off-site learning experiences
• Engaging parents, members of business, or community volunteers to provide alternative activities or enrichment programs.

Time Strategy #2: Restructured or Rescheduled Time

Restructured time involves formally altering the time frame of the traditional calendar, school day, or teaching schedule. While such interventions involve attention to a variety of practical problems, — bus schedules, parent schedules, child care, traditional summer activities, and children from one family enrolled in several schools — these strategies require more formal commitment and participation from stakeholders, particularly from parents, administrators, and school boards.

Following are approaches for altering time frames.
• "Banking" time, has become a common scheduling option in both elementary and secondary schools. Many schools adjust schedules to create time for teachers to plan and collaborate by accruing hours that are applied to students' early dismissal or in some cases late arrival. A middle school banked time accrued by eliminating the daily 10-minute homeroom. By assigning homeroom tasks to the first period teacher, sufficient time was accumulated for conversion into six half-day early dismissals. Another district rearranged the daily schedule by adding student time on

four days and facilitating the early release of students on the fifth day of the week. A variation of banking time for another school involved shaving five or 10 minutes from lunch periods. Still other schools add a number of minutes to the daily schedule in exchange for a monthly planning day. Whatever the configuration, banking creates time for use in collaborating, parent conferencing, and participating in professional development activities.

• Creating a first period prior to the arrival of students is yet another model for creating time for teachers to interact. By delaying the students' day, teachers are afforded a common time for planning and collaborating while they are fresh and energized.

• Implementing a form of parallel block scheduling yields additional time for professional planning and interaction. Under this time strategy, classes meet for five periods on Monday, Tuesday, Thursday, and Friday. On those four days, three periods are scheduled before lunch and two periods after lunch. On Wednesdays, only four class periods are held, and there is no lunch break. Students are dismissed after the fourth class to provide the faculty a student-free, two-hour block of planning time.

• Structuring "schools within a school" provides more flexibility in scheduling time. This strategy affords schools options to address time demands by adjusting schedules, calendars, and structures within a building.

Time Strategy #3: Common Time

Some schools are using the "common" planning time concept to create working time to support restructuring programs, interdisciplinary teams, discipline or subject area collaboration, and grade level planning. While "prep periods" are not uncommon, they are not sufficient. The concept of school transformation is evolving from what individual teachers do in individual classrooms to the acceptance of the critical need for teacher collaboration and the development of collegiality or "facultyness." Many schools, therefore, are experimenting with ways to schedule "common" planning time among colleagues with similar assignments.

The following is an ex-

ample of a middle school framework designed for implementing effective common planning time blocks.

During reorganization, most teachers' rooms were moved, enabling teams to be located near each other. The next reorganization involved the time schedule. With a flexible block schedule, all passing times were eliminated, yielding an additional 29 minutes daily. Additionally, by shaving five minutes from the daily homeroom period, 34 minutes were gained. Applied to six days in the schedule, this produced a total gain of 204 minutes.

This allowed each team one 47-minute planning period with additional time for student activity periods, tutorials, snack breaks, or student committee meetings.

Time Strategy #4:
Better-Used Time

Faculties engaged in school restructuring are examining ways to use currently scheduled meetings and professional development activities more effectively by focusing on planning and collaboration, rather than on administration or information dissemination. Although many schools now convene regular faculty meetings that incorporate some form of professional development activity, too frequently these assemblages continue to be autocratic and emphasize administrivia. While teachers express a strong desire for more planning time and for opportunities to grow and learn professionally, faculty meetings continue to be viewed as wasteful of their time.

Innovative strategies currently being implemented include:
• Allocating all pre-opening workdays for teacher planning and preparation
• Reducing/eliminating administrivia at faculty meetings through improved methods for communication, leadership rotation, reallocation of agenda setting, use of a management council (Note: faculty meetings are specifically designated for talking, thinking, sharing, and reflecting on substantive issues. Memos and a teacher bulletin board with daily postings are used for information dissemination.)
• Shifting from repetitive, yearly, summative evaluations to multi-year, formative, professional growth opportunities
• Having single-issue faculty meetings moderated by an elected faculty member
• Networking information among school personnel through a local computerized Email system by equipping each staff member with a computer on his/her desk
• Restricting time required for nonprofessional duties.

Time Strategy #5:
Purchased Time

Obviously, when funding permits, additional teachers, clerks, parents, support staff can be hired, class size reduced, and planning periods expanded. When faced with budget constraints, however, many schools have designed creative ways for purchasing time that deserve review.

Innovative "purchasing" practices include:
• Establishing a "substi-

Where Do You Find the Time?

Following are five strategies that educators across the country are using to find more time.

1. *Freed-Up Time:* Using various arrangements to free teachers from direct student supervision. These include enlisting administrators to teach classes, authorizing teaching assistants and college interns to teach classes at regular intervals under the direction of a teacher, and teaming teachers in a way that allows one teacher to instruct for another.

2. *Restructured Time:* Formally altering the time frame of the traditional calendar, school day, or teaching schedule

3. *Common Time:* Using common planning time to support restructuring programs, interdisciplinary teams, subject-area collaboration, and grade-level planning

4. *Better-Used Time:* Using currently scheduled meetings and professional development activities more effectively by focusing on planning and collaboration

5. *Purchased Time:* Hiring additional teachers, clerks, parents, and support staff to allow for smaller class sizes and/or expanded or additional planning sessions.

tute bank" of 30 to 40 days per year from which teachers withdraw time to participate in committee work, to engage in special professional development activities, and to provide support to other development projects

• Writing grant proposals to foundations or other funding agencies to secure

The real issue is not just adding or manipulating time, but changing the fundamental way we do business.

monies to pay for early release time for the faculty to plan and prepare

• Using district-allocated staff development funds to pay stipends to teachers for summer planning time

• Negotiating bargaining agreements that provide extra-duty pay or compensation for evening/summer planning activities

• Receiving "in-service" credits from the district for personal time devoted to the development of new programs.

Changing the Way We Do Business!

Following a review of the time dilemmas facing school personnel and suggestions posed for short-term and immediate relief, it is the Committee's strong contention that real solutions to this complex and vexing issue must be conceived in a new and different context. The real issue is not just adding or manipulating time, but changing the fundamental way we do business.

The Committee strongly believes the Association must approach the time issue with creative and flexible thinking and action. The Committee fully recognizes the frustration the time dilemma inflicts on school personnel and the natural tendency to question the various time solutions. However, if the Association's efforts are largely engaged in simply warding off unwanted intrusions, little time and energy will remain to create new school and professional environments that focus attention on the underlying systemic solutions.

This restructured role for the Association envisioned by the Committee focuses on the control of time rather than on the amount of time. The public debate on adding extra hours to the school day or

days to the school calendar is shallow dialogue if divorced from the several fundamental concepts of the use and control of time in American schools.

This section of the Committee's report sets forth five, long-term, integrated strategies aimed at reconstructing how time is controlled. These strategies are as follows:

I. New Roles for Teachers

The conceptualization of what teaching is has been shaped by traditions from the past. Schools today are a reflection of the organizational theories of Frederick Taylor and scientific management. Teachers as well as other "touch workers" on the bottom of the organizational pyramid, were expected to be "doers." Planning, decision making, problem solving, and other "managerial" functions were reserved for higher levels of the organization. "Teacher-proof" pedagogy and curriculum were determined by the decision makers.

Teachers were viewed as workers; students as products. The pedagogy promoted the doctrine. Students were generally put into passive learning environments with teachers and textbooks delivering the content information. In such a conception of schooling, teachers' work could really only take place with students. Teachers were expected to correct papers, conference with parents, and handle other "duties" (e.g., bathroom and hall monitoring, parking lot supervision, school-picture money collection). The teachers' role, however, was conceived as being "on the job" only when direct student contact was involved.

The educational reform movement is turning the factory-school concept on its head. This parallels private sector organizational change espoused by Deming, Senge, and Covey. As early as 1978, researchers concluded that teacher involvement was necessary for implementing and sustaining school change. (Berman and McLaughlin, 1978) It is increasingly obvious that school reform cannot be undertaken successfully without the participation of the "touch workers." It just does not work to expect experts and administrators to do the planning and make all the decisions and then require teachers and other school employees to implement the plans.

Research concludes that collaborative time among teachers and other school personnel is essential in sustaining reflectiveness and collective self-examination so necessary for effective functioning, self-renewal, and reform. Raywid commented, "The case for regular, frequent, and sustained collegial interaction time for teachers is being made from several different research perspectives, and such time is being asserted as important to the accomplishment of several different purposes: successful school change and improvement; sustaining a good school and facilitating the professional growth of individual teachers; and enabling schools to remain capable of self-renewal." (Raywid, 1991)

The current fallacy is not the recognition of this need for new professional responsibilities of teachers, but the false assumption that the original roles and functions of teachers can be left in place while adding the new duties of being partners in the change process. What is called for is recognition that the definition of teachers' work is much broader than standing in front of a classroom. Failure to do this places responsibility for systemic school reform on the backs of teachers' own time.

In a recent study of Asian schools, one of the greatest differences found was the amount of time teachers had for planning, preparing lessons, and other professional responsibilities. One author of the study reported:

Beijing teachers were incredulous after we described a typical day in American schools. When, they asked, did the teachers prepare their lessons, consult with one another about teaching techniques, grade the students' papers, and work with individual students who were having difficulties? Beijing teachers, they explained, are responsible for classes for no more than three hours a day; for those with homeroom duties, the total is four hours a day. The situation is similar in Japan and Taiwan, where, according to our estimates, teachers are in charge of classes only 60 percent of the time they are at school. (Stevenson, 1992)

A teacher who recently visited and studied schools in Western and Eastern Europe informed the Committee that teachers in Europe average 18 hours of direct classroom instruction per week. In many cases, in West Germany, Belarus, Ukraine, Moldavia, and Russia this average represents a six-day school week. In contrast, American teachers average 25 hours of direct classroom instruction during a five-day school week. (Nelson, 1993)

An example of efforts to reapportion the time allocated for classroom and professional development in this country exists in the Wells School District in Maine. The local association and the school district have approved a 10-year strategic plan. One component of the plan includes the goal that by the year 2000, a minimum of 50 percent of a teacher's work time will be in direct contact with students; the other 50 percent will be in pursuing other professional responsibilities.

The Committee Recommends

1. that the National Education Association endorse the policy that the role of the teacher be restructured so at least one-half of the contract time be for professional responsibilities and one-half for direct contact with students.

2. that the communication and media vehicles of the NEA carry articles and other messages designed to promote a restructured role for classroom teachers.

3. that bargaining contract language, designed to facilitate these new role definitions, be prepared and disseminated to affiliates. Such language should not suggest deducting new needed time functions from teachers' personal lives (e.g., weekends and holidays), even with compensation. To compensate for this time actually reinforces the old paradigm, although the Committee obviously does not support uncompensated time.

What is needed is a reconceptualization of professional time for teachers, with a professional salary commensurate with their responsibilities.

4. that training be provided for both leaders and staff to implement these new time strategies. Such training should be an integrated part of the normal training program offerings of the NEA.

II. Teacher Control Of Time

One of the realities of schools today is that curriculum and learning are designed to fit time parameters, rather than time parameters designed to fit learning. As one teacher commented, "The schedule is god." Educators readily acknowledge that some students take three minutes to learn a concept that other students take 30 minutes or possibly three hours to learn. Yet the common school structure makes time constant and learning the variable. The better pattern would be for learning to be the constant and time the variable. To implement this almost radical idea, teachers would have to be afforded more authority to control learning time, because only at the individual student learning level could such decisions be made.

Obviously, this line of reasoning incurs panic in efficiency experts who are trying to manipulate schedules for hundreds to thousands of students in a school or school district. Current school schedules, however, often obstruct learning and teaching, rather than enhance it. The Committee believes control of learning time should be decentralized to the site level.

Another issue of time control is the concept of "colonization of time." Hargreaves defines colonization as the process where administrators subsume or "colonize" teachers' time for their own purposes. There is growing evidence that a struggle is underway between teachers and administrators over control of backstage time (e.g., private reflection and collegial discussions, personal planning as opposed to front stage time defined as "on stage" in front of the classroom). For preparation time, in particular, a key issue is whether teachers will be empowered to exercise professional discretion to use time backstage or front stage as they see fit, or will such preparation time be colonized by administrators for their purposes. (Hargreaves, 1990)

The Committee concludes that new roles for teachers and control of time are interrelated and mutually necessary.

The Committee Recommends

1. that the National Education Association advocate the control of teaching and learning time be vested with local faculties at the site level. Such advocacy should be incorporated into policy resolutions and be given visibility through NEA's media and communications functions.

2. that affiliates seek to strengthen teachers' and other school employees' control of time for both learning and other professional purposes through appropriate legislative and bargaining processes.

III. Coordination of School and Community Resources

Over the years schools have been compelled to accept increasing responsibility for helping to meet the noninstructional needs of children (e.g., medical, counseling, nutritional needs). As society and the family structure have changed, the problems students bring to school have increased in number and become more diverse and complex. Teachers are confronted daily with the time demands of these problems.

While the schools must continue to contribute their fair share for aiding these children, it must be recognized that the more attention schools are asked to devote to noninstructional needs, the less time they have to provide quality education for all students.

Schools are the natural focal point in the community for reaching children and young adults. But as educators, we must also insist that other community, social, and governmental agencies accept responsibility for aiding in the development and learning of the whole child.

All problems affecting students' ability to learn must be resolved by school/community collaboration and coordination and not be left entirely to the schools.

While the schools have a responsibility to encourage these other agencies and resources to work together to ensure efficient coordination of services and the accountability for the safety of children, educators must have the help and support of the community to achieve their mission. Such cooperation can also stimulate needed community support to help in the learning activities of the schools.

The Committee Recommends

1. that the National Education Association re-endorse Principle # Eight of The NEA Agenda for Excellence, which calls for the coordination of community resources in the schools for the benefit of students.

2. that the NEA Center for Teaching and Learning prepare and distribute examples of community involvement in schools.

IV. Standard Contract Year for School Employees

The Committee believes the standard for the profession should be a 12-month contract year, as opposed to the current practice of a nine-or 10-month standard. The new expectations and time demands for practitioner participation in restructuring schools and the recognition of the need for increased quality professional development time strongly argue for making the standard contract year for teachers and other school employees 12 months, as opposed to the traditional student year. The Association should state clearly that as a profession we seek negotiated salary, paid vacation time, and options. Such a contract year must be a part of the bargaining contract.

In current practice in school districts across the country, the standard or typical contract year for teachers and other school employees is the student school year, plus a few days for inservice/professional development activities. What is being referenced here is not the schedule for disbursement of paychecks. Many districts offer "12-month contracts," but these only take the nine-or 10-month contract year and stretch paychecks to be distributed over a 12-month time frame.

The consequences of the current practice of the typical contract year are often negative and time confining. Despite how educators interpret their work year, the reality is that educators and other school employees are "laid off" without pay for one to three months each year. The myth that teachers "only work nine months a year and a six-hour day" is destructive for seeking improved compensation and for garnering increased public support for public education. Many educators augment their salary throughout the school year, and especially during the summer months, because the opportunity to work for increased compensa-

tion within the profession is not an option.

The option called for by the Committee acknowledges that some teachers, needing to pursue professional goals, may not seek a full 12-month contract. The Committee also acknowledges that the transition to a standard 12-month contract for teachers will be hampered by lack of funds. These two circumstances may ease any transition period. The Committee believes, nevertheless, that the option for a full 12-month contract for all teachers is both logical and professionally strategic and should be an explicit goal of the Association.

The achievement of this goal would enable schools to have more flexibility in determining decisions concerning the

length and configuration of the student school year, in planning and developing new curriculum offerings, and in providing professional development time for educators. Additionally, opportunities for remedial and enrichment programs for students and large blocks of uninterrupted collegial, professional planning time would be significantly enhanced. Thus, the 12-month year establishes a new framework for meaningful discussions about student learning time and teacher professional time. Additionally, it changes the focus from discussion of time to the more appropriate topics of curriculum, instruction, and assessment.

One important caveat is necessary at this point. While expanded opportunities for concentrated pe-

riods of planning are very beneficial, it would be unwise to assume such time could be a substitute for planning time during the school day. It is very important that teachers and other school personnel be provided opportunity for reflection and dialogue on daily events, enabling them to make needed adjustments and

---

Five Timely Goals

As educators, we need to seek:

- Building-level control of teaching and learning time

- Coordination of school and community resources to better serve students

- Increased access to technology that enables efficient use of time (specifically, to telephones and computers)

- Restructuring of teachers' work time so they spend 50 percent of their time teaching classes and 50 percent on expanded professional responsibilities

- A standard 12-month contract year with a negotiated salary, paid vacation time, and options for all teachers to work a nine-month year if they choose.

corrections in the plans as implementation progresses. The Committee recommendations for new roles

Today, curriculum and learning are designed to fit time parameters, rather than time parameters designed to fit learning.

for teachers are fully consistent with an expanded standard contract year.

The Committee Recommends

1. that the National Education Association go on record calling for a standard 12-month contract year with a negotiated salary, paid vacation time, and options for all teachers and other school personnel. Appropriate attention must also be given to upgrading structural facilities for year round work and learning.

2. that the NEA provide strategies, options, and support to staff for a 12-month contract year for use by affiliates in bargaining. In collective bargaining states, an appropriate vehicle must exist to ensure that collective bargaining occurs. In nonbargaining states, legislation must ensure that as the contract year for employees increases, salaries increase on a prorata basis.

V. Virtual Time to Enhance the Professional Role of School Personnel

The NEA has previously called for the use of technology to enhance the professional life of teachers and to ease the burden of paperwork. (*Educational Technology*, 1989, and *Educational Telecommunications*, 1992) The NEA reports call for a computer on every teacher's desk and a telephone in every classroom. There is overwhelming evidence that technology can ease the time burden in schoolwork. Few other work environments are as technologically backward as the schools in America. Even grocery store clerks and service workers in food and retail industries have access to technology to make their task more manageable and efficient.

Following guidelines and policies previously set forth by NEA, the Committee believes that the expanded use of technology for both the professional use of educators and for teaching shall have significant benefits in helping teachers and other school personnel better manage their time.

The Committee Recommends

1. that the NEA reaffirm its support for telephones and computers in classrooms for the professional use of educators.

2. that the NEA fully develop the NEA Online electronic network to facilitate communication among NEA members.

Summary

The clamor to revitalize the nation's schools is reverberating across the land. Time-bound educators, grappling daily with societal problems, budgetary constraints, burgeoning knowledge and skill demands for students to master, accountability and standards' requirements, must now add active participation in school reform to their already onerous responsibilities. Time limitations are impacting the working lives of teachers and other school employees and inhibiting change efforts. "Until teachers and other school staff are provided significantly more time and resources, they can't give today's troubled children the attention they need to become tomorrow's educated and caring adults." (Geiger, 1993)

The remedies, while complex, are time-based. Reconceptualization of time is an imperative for schools to restructure to better serve the needs of children. Because comprehensive, lasting reform can only occur when school employees are cen-

tral to the change efforts, resolution of the time issue is one of the most crucial problems confronting educators today.

The Committee believes the Association must assume an advocacy leadership role in the time issue. Such advocacy not only puts the NEA at the forefront of educational restructuring, but also provides NEA members with critical support in their efforts to resolve crucial time dilemmas. Time must become a significant focus at the bargaining table, at legislative exchanges, at budget debates, at parent discussion groups, and at all other forums with constituencies concerned with student achievement. IT IS ABOUT TIME!

References

• Agenda for Excellence. 1985. "An Open Letter to America on Schools, Students, and Tomorrow." Washington, D.C.: National Education Association.

• Berman, P., and Mc Laughlin, M. 1978. "Federal Programs Supporting Educational Change." In *Implementing and Sustaining Innovations*. Santa Monica, Calif.: Rand.

• Covey, S. R. 1989. *The Seven Habits of Highly Effective People*. New York: Fireside.

• Deming, W. E. 1981-82. "Improvement of Quality and Productivity Through Action by Management." *National Productivity Review*, 1: 12-22. Winter.

• Firestone, W., and Rosenblum, S. 1988. "The Alienation and Commitment of Students and Teachers in Urban High Schools: A Conceptual Framework." *Educational Evaluation and Policy Quarterly*, 10: 285-300.

• Geiger, K. 1993. "Inside an American Classroom: The Realities of Children and Schools." *The Washington Post*, May 16, p. C4.

• Grenzke, J. M. 1993. *Our Children's Schools: Are They Good Enough?* Hartford, Conn.: Connecticut Education Association.

• Hargreaves, A. 1990. "Teachers' Work and the Politics of Time and Space." *Qualitative Studies in Education*, 3(4) :3150

• Little, J. W. 1984. "Norms of Collegiality and Experimentation: Conditions for School Success." *American Education Research Journal*, 19: 325-40.

• Louis, K. S., and Smith, B. 1990. "Teachers' Work: Current Issues and Prospects for Reform." In P. Reyes (ed.), *Productivity and Performance in Educational Organizations*,

23-47. Newbury Park, Calif.: Sage.

• National Education Association Special Committee Report. 1989. *Educational Technology*. Washington, D.C.

• National Education Association Special Committee Report on Telecommunications. 1992. *Educational Telecommunications*. Washington, D.C.

• Nelson, J. 1993. Interview conducted April 29.

• Price, H. B. 1993. "Teacher Professional Development: It's About Time." *Education Week*, May 12, pp. 24,32.

• Prager, K. 1992. "Collaborative Planning Time for Teachers." *Brief to Principals No. 2*. Center on Organization and Restructuring of Schools. Madison, Wis.: Winter.

• Purnell, S., and Hill, P.

1992. *Time for Reform*. Santa Monica, Calif.: Rand.

• Raywid, M. A. 1991. Making Time to Do Reform, unpublished paper, pp. 5.

• Rosenholtz, S. J. 1989. *Teachers' Workplace: The Social Organization of Schools*. New York: Longman.

• Senge, P. 1990. *The Fifth Discipline*. New York: Doubleday.

• Sommerfeld, M. 1993. "Time and Space." *Education Week*, March 13, pp. 13-19.

• Stevenson, H. 1992. "Learning from Asian Schools." *Scientific American*, December, pp. 74-75.

• Watts, G. D., and Castle, S. 1992. "Electronic Networking and the Construction of Professional Knowledge." *Phi Delta Kappan*: 684-89. ◆

Reader Reflections

Insights: _____

_____

_____

_____

_____

_____

Actions for Our School (District) to Consider: _____

_____

_____

_____

_____

_____

_____

_____

_____

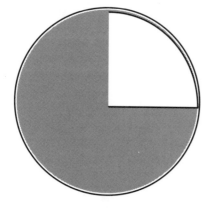

BUILDING TIME INTO THE SCHOOL YEAR

Working together, our association and district developed a number of ways to save time so that teachers could be free to work on school restructuring projects.

For the last few years, I have been a library media specialist at Pinellas Technical Education Center in Pinellas County, Florida. Before that, I was a media specialist at other schools as well as a high school English teacher and a middle school teacher. Throughout my 17-year career in education, it seems I have never had enough time to do everything that needed doing, either personally or professionally.

The problem compounded in 1988, though, when I became a member of the newly formed Summit Committee, which was a joint restructuring venture of the Pinellas Classroom Teachers Association and the Pinellas School District. Co-chaired by then-superintendent Scott Rose and association president Don Macneale, the committee was a first step in working together to redesign education and facilitate change in Pinellas County. Committee members included teachers, support personnel, district- and building-level administrators, and teacher association staff. The work was exciting, but extremely time-consuming.

Then in 1990, Pinellas was chosen as the National Education Association's Florida Learning Lab site, and through this project, we continued to expand on our restructuring work.

More and more, we faced the problem of TIME. Students were in school for six or more hours, teachers worked a seven-and-a-half hour day (and then some!), and the state was mandating increasing numbers of programs and paperwork that had to fit within that time frame. So, how could we ask teachers to assume even more tasks—to take on the time-consuming responsibilities involved in restructuring and running their schools? We decided we couldn't, unless we found ways to

LINDA A. BACON
Library Media Specialist
Pinellas Technical Education Center
Pinellas County, Florida

build time for this into the school year.

Working together, the teacher association and district developed a number of approaches to saving time so that teachers could be free to work on school restructuring projects. Joint committees worked on identifying ways to eliminate paperwork and duplication of effort at the school level. Administrators were asked to work on eliminating or shortening building-level meetings. Schools were encouraged to redesign master schedules and school calendars in a way that alloted time to work on restructuring efforts within the school day.

Five specific innovations that were, and continue to be, particularly effective in building time into the school year are as follows:

Innovation #1: Substitute Days

When our staff got together to brainstorm the problem of dividing up supplemental responsibilities at the school (clubs, science fair, committees, etc.), we agreed that the supplemental money provided by the county for these tasks didn't begin to compensate us for the time we spent performing them. Adding to this time problem was the fact that our fundamental magnet program mandated four parent conferences a year with each parent — talk about a time drain! The consensus was that the supplemental money really wasn't as important as the time needed to accomplish the various tasks we faced.

Our solution was a unique approach to paying supplements and using time. We prioritized the "extra" jobs that needed to be done at school; these were distributed among all teachers, with those of us not having direct classroom responsibilities taking on a heavier load than classroom teachers. The major portion of the supplemental funds was then used to pay for time: We bought substitutes.

Each classroom teacher was given a substitute for two release days that could be taken in full- or half-day increments. Teachers could use these days to conduct parent conferences, work on supplemental tasks (setting up the science fair, layout of the yearbook, etc.), or to do other tasks related to school improvement. There was also a small, discretionary amount of money available to buy additional substitutes for special projects as needed. Parents were supportive of the plan, and teachers really appreciated the time this freed up for them to work on a variety of projects and responsibilities.

Innovation #2: Early Release Days

One of our most effective ways of finding more time

> *Our main problem with implementing time innovations in a district our size has been with "buy-in" from all the stakeholders.*

in the district came when we got the school board to adopt a calendar that included four Early Release days, spread throughout the year. On these days, schools run on a shortened schedule and students go home three hours early. After the students leave, school staffs can then meet to work on school improvement. While the county council of PTAs was initially opposed to this idea, we convinced them that the time would be well spent by staffs by designating these large blocks of time for training, planning, and implementing school improvement projects.

The shortened days gained particular significance with the passage of the Florida Education Reform and Accountability Act, also called Blueprint 2000. Suddenly, schools

were faced with developing school improvement plans, participating in massive amounts of training, and working with all stakeholders in the school community (parents, businesses, community members, etc.). Teachers still faced the same amount of time for instruction, the same workday length, and no additional funds while they were developing these plans. It became more important than ever for us to have large blocks of time for working together.

Blueprint 2000 outlines seven goals for schools to meet in order to prepare students for the twenty-first century, with standards and outcomes for each goal. At my current school, Pinellas Technical Education Center-Clearwater (PTEC), we have used the Early Release

About Pinellas County School District...

The Pinellas County School District is the seventh largest school district in Florida, with more than 96,000 students in 79 elementary, 22 middle, and 15 high schools. In addition, we have five exceptional education centers, two discipline centers, seven community schools, three adult education centers, and two technical education centers. Pinellas ranks twenty-second in size out of more than 16,000 districts in the U.S.

Located on the west-central coast of Florida, the Pinellas district serves a growing urban area and boasts one of the better salary schedules in the state. The district serves students from a variety of cultural backgrounds, ranging from a large Greek community in the northern part of the county to a growing Asian-American population in south county as well as a large African-American population in mid- and south county; minority groups comprise around 12% of the student population in Pinellas schools.

Pinellas also boasts a variety of educational programs outside of the traditional K-12 offerings. Pinellas supports the largest public school International Baccalaureate class in the world, with 91 students in the class of 1994. Other innovative programs include a Center for Advanced Technologies at Lakewood High School, a performing arts magnet program, a math/science/technology magnet program at K-8 Bay Point School; five partnership schools with area businesses; dropout prevention programs at the elementary, middle, and high school levels; and several other special programs. Pinellas also offers programs within the regular school for students with various exceptionalities. The average teacher-pupil ratio (TPR) for the 1993-94 school year is 1:23 for kindergarten, 1:24 for first through third grade, and 1:29 for grades four and five. TPRs vary according to subject within middle and high schools.

days to develop and implement our school improvement plan to meet these goals.

PTEC has used a variety of techniques on the shortened days to gather data and provide training. We have used large-group

Our schools are free to try a variety of approaches in dealing with time, rather than be locked into a "district model."

presentations and small-group brainstorming sessions. Groups have focused on the "big picture" and on how Blueprint 2000 will impact their daily work.

For example, we spent one day identifying the impact of Blueprint 2000

within work groups. I facilitated a meeting where a work group brainstormed the issues of how BP 2000 affects our students, program, and staff; what strategies we can implement to meet the goals; and what outcomes we want to achieve. We prioritized the seven goals as they related to our departments and identified impacts, strategies, and outcomes for each. The information gathered on this and other shortened days, and the data from a school improvement needs assessment, were used to develop the school improvement plan that we submitted the following spring.

Currently, I am serving on a process team at PTEC that is determining how to use this year's shortened days. One of

our goals in our school improvement plan is to provide staff members with the necessary training to implement continual quality improvement in the classroom, to use mastery learning and performance-based assessment, and to help teachers improve their skills in their areas of certification. On our first shortened day, we are planning a needs assessment activity that will involve the entire staff in brainstorming training needs. We will use the data gathered on that day to develop our training plans for the other shortened days this year.

The key to the success of the shortened days has been the fact that school staffs decide how to use them to meet their specific needs. Early Release days have worked so well

that this year we incorporated six days into the calendar.

Innovation #3: Fewer and More Efficient Meetings

As I mentioned earlier, during the last few years we have been working very hard in the district to reduce the number of in-school meetings that are conducted. This has been more successful at some schools than at others. But with the increased need for training in school-improvement processes and curriculum innovations, freeing up this time has been a priority for the district.

At my last school, faculty meetings were conducted twice a month and consisted mostly of the principal talking or reading lists of announcements to us. But at PTEC, if we don't have at least two items submitted for the agenda ahead of time, we don't have a staff meeting that month. The lead association building representative compiles the agenda from items submitted by teachers, support personnel, and/or administrators on a form that we developed for that purpose. Each person who submits an item indicates the amount of time he or she will need and is obliged to maintain that time limit. We try to stay within a 40-minute time frame for the entire meeting. By the way, routine announcements are taboo at these meetings. We communicate that info through a weekly bulletin that each staff member receives or through special memos that we place in staffers' mailboxes.

Innovation #4: TDE Days

Another way that the district has tried to provide time for training and school improvement is through the use of TDE (Temporary Duty Elsewhere) days. A TDE is official permission for a staff member to be out of his or her regular work site and still on the district payroll; the staff member does not have to use sick leave or personal time, is covered by Workman's Compensation, and is provided with a substitute.

In Pinellas, training is often scheduled for large groups of teachers from around the district; for example, the High Success Network has conducted several workshops in the district during the last few years. But this has caused additional prob-

lems that we didn't anticipate. Occasionally, there have been so many teachers attending training sessions at the same time that the district has run out of substitutes.

Last year, in a district with around 6,000 teachers, we used so many TDEs for workshops and other activities that the district and association set up a task force to deal with the problem of providing adequate numbers of substitutes. The task force made recommendations on scheduling large-scale training sessions to avoid this problem and set up a master calendar for scheduling and balancing TDEs throughout the district. Each school is also urged to plan carefully as it provides TDEs for staff members to work on school improvement or attend conferences.

Prime Time Innovations

At Pinellas, we use the following innovations to build in time for working on school-improvement efforts.

☐ **Substitute Days**

☐ **Early Release Days**

☐ **Fewer and More Efficient Meetings**

☐ **Temporary-Duty-Elsewhere (TDE) Days**

☐ **Professional Education (ProEd) Days**

Innovation #5: ProEd Days

As in many districts, Pinellas has Professional Education (ProEd) days built into the calendar. These days are used for districtwide workshops and the traditional end-of-semester planning days. This year, schools had a new option related to these days and the issue of time. They could choose to move one or more of these days before the beginning or after the end of the school year to use for training or other planned activities that could not be done in smaller time blocks. Then on the ProEd days, these teachers would not work.

nized), but it has also given us the freedom to try lots of new ideas. It has provided a waiver process that frees us from many of the old state and local mandates so that we can be more flexible in our use of time.

in school; we worked very hard to convince them that this time for teachers and staffs was very valuable. The students have adjusted to the variety of schedules and calendars quite easily; however, we need to be collecting more data on how they are impacted by these changes and the impact on community groups such as day-care centers, recreational programs, and so on.

pate in improving education.

I have seen us move from a system where teachers were constantly attending mandated meetings at both the school and district level, to a system where teachers now control the use of their time outside the classroom.

Evaluation

Have all of these innovations worked? I guess I would answer with a qualified "yes." We have experienced success and failure in a variety of ways. Blueprint 2000 has turned a spotlight on education in Florida (our every move is scruti-

Our main problem with implementing these innovations in a district this size has been with "buy-in" from all the stakeholders. As I stated earlier, parents were initially opposed to shortening the time their children were

Teachers in the district have not all been eager to embrace the time innovations. These innovations have required increased effort and time to plan staff activities, and not everyone wants to participate in training or team activities. But many teachers have welcomed the opportunity to help shape their work environment and actively participate in improving education.

Then, too, while there is commitment to these efforts at the highest district levels, some building-level administrators have not been able to make the adjustment to letting their staffs actively participate in making these decisions.

While the innovations mentioned are part of local policy, negotiated contract, and/or Blueprint 2000, change still comes slowly. We have been more successful in some schools than others and are seeing constant progress as teachers and administrators gain the confidence and trust to try new things.

In addition, Pinellas is involved in a new type of collaborative bargaining that is working to solve some of these problems.

Future Plans

Because our program for time use is so diverse, it is hard to predict where we'll go from here. One of the strengths of our program is that almost anything goes: Schools are free to try a variety of approaches in dealing with this issue, rather than being locked into a "district model." Currently, we're working at the local level to add four more shortened ProEd days to the calendar so that we will have one each month. On the state level, we are working to have the state fund an additional five days on the teacher calendar, to be used for school improvement planning and training.

We are making progress in using time more wisely in Pinellas, but we know we still have a long way to go. In the 11 years I have taught in Pinellas, I have seen us move from a system where teachers were constantly attending mandated meetings at both the school and district level, to a system where teachers now control the use of their time outside the classroom. I feel a sense of accomplishment and power knowing that my time is valued and is being used for activities that will benefit me professionally as well as my school and my students. ◆

Advice for Using Time Strategies

1 Develop a cooperative relationship between the school district and your teachers association in order to work together on innovative projects. Let the district see that the association does more than just bargain for salaries.

2 Bargain flexible contract language that will allow teachers to develop innovative programs at the school level, including innovations in time use.

3 Develop a joint mission statement for the association and district: A shared vision or "constancy of purpose" is necessary for success.

4 Encourage people to take risks, and set up an environment where it's OK to fail; emphasize learning from your mistakes. This was one of the original guidelines developed by Pinnellas's Summit Committee, and it led to a lot of innovations.

5 Encourage each school to develop a plan that meets its particular needs; what works at one school doesn't necessarily work at another. Shortened days may be great for some schools; block scheduling may suit others; while buying time may be the answer at a third.

6 Get lots of input from your stakeholders on how this innovation will affect each group. Use good decision-making processes to develop your plan.

7 Don't do things for the sake of change alone or just to make your working conditions better. Every change should be made in the context of: "How can we improve education for kids?"

8 Prioritize: Realize that you will *never* have enough time to do everything you want to do. Start talking from the very beginning about what you can stop doing so that you have time to do the things that really need to be done.

9 Provide training in meeting management, decision-making, teamwork, and so on.

Reader Reflections

Insights: _____

_____

_____

_____

_____

Actions for Our School (District) to Consider: _____

_____

_____

_____

_____

_____

_____

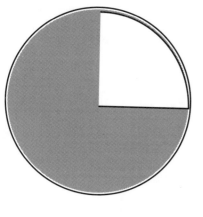

WE COULD NOT GO ANY FASTER

We decided that if we restructured the school day into fewer, longer time blocks, maybe we could find the time to do all the teaching and planning we needed to do.

Time—to teach, to demonstrate, to reteach, to teach differently, to involve students

Time—to learn, to experience, to relearn, to learn differently, to process and practice with guidance

Time—to appreciate, to reflect

Time—to restructure, to solve the problems of too little time!

In 1989, when a core group of the Wasson High School faculty formed the Restructuring Committee, we concluded that breaking the old paradigm of seven 50-minute classes a day would best serve as the foundation for significant school reform, reform that we hoped would increase student success.

The way we saw it, the district dictated the length of the school day (bus schedule) and the school year; the district controlled graduation requirements and mandated some uniformity in course offerings and outlines. But, at the building level, we could control what actually happened during the school day.

We decided that if we restructured the day into fewer, yet longer time blocks, maybe we could find the time in and out of class to do all the teaching, reteaching, learning, involving, reflecting, restructuring, and problem solving we

PATRICIA GRAHAM

English Teacher

Wasson High School

Colorado Springs, Colorado

desperately needed, yet somehow never had the time to do, for our students and ourselves.

And so, in response to the frustrations of students, parents, and teachers; to the changing needs of our student population and the post-secondary educational scene; and to the desires of the faculty to do an even better job of teaching; we created the Wasson Block Schedule.

Background

Before I tell you more about this schedule, I'd like to give you some background on our school. Opened in 1959 in

Colorado Springs, Colorado, Wasson High School is one of five regular high schools in the fourth largest school district in the state (about

Four key ingredients came together to make the work of the Restructuring Committee successful—climate, ownership, focus, and communication....

33,000 students in 1993-94). Wasson had long had a reputation for high standards; academic excellence; and a traditional, primarily college-preparatory curriculum with enough vocational and elective programs to be

the typical comprehensive three-year high school.

Classes met for 50 minutes each day, with seven periods in a single school day. Students averaged five classes per day, but seven was not unusual, particularly for honors/AP students and for students who had failed required courses. Teachers taught five of the seven periods and had 30 to 35 students in each class. Most courses were two semesters in length, with one credit awarded for each one-period, one-semester class. On a daily basis, students typically dealt with five to seven teachers and five to seven sets of homework; teachers dealt with as many as 175 students and five preparations.

Nothing seemed glaringly wrong—we looked like most other high

schools—but by the 1988-89 school year, a majority of the faculty felt the frustrations of being isolated from our peers, of engaging increasingly apathetic students, and of not being able to provide desired innovations and individualization. Not content to accept the status quo, and more than a little alarmed that we no longer felt the same excitement about teaching, the Wasson faculty formed the Restructuring Committee in September of 1989, with our principal's blessings. The committee's purpose was to increase staff awareness of the need for and possibility of change, to coach the staff through the process of change, to pinpoint our greatest controllable frustrations, to study solutions to the time issues, and to propose a new master schedule.

Process

Four key ingredients came together to make the work of the Restructuring Committee successful—climate, ownership, focus, and communication—and from our experience, we would suggest that they are all essential.

Climate

Our administrators did not set up road blocks, as some have done in other schools. They actually created a positive climate for change. They encouraged and facilitated the change by fostering and participating in open exchanges of ideas in small and large staff meetings and in the faculty lounge, by financially and psychologically supporting the committee's work through funding visitations and teaching classes to free teachers to work on

Student Comparisons

	Previous Wasson Schedule	Wasson Block Schedule
Periods Per Day	7	4
Average Number of Classes Per Day	5	4
Time Per Class	50 min.	90 min.

committee, by covering printing costs, by fighting battles at the district level, and by valuing what the staff and the committee developed.

Ownership

Our work was totally teacher-initiated, directed, and based. The building-level administrative team were facilitators; they empowered the staff, clarified issues, provided resources, and helped put the process in place. But the committee was the change agent. A teacher chaired the 11-member committee composed of nine teachers and two administrators, one of whom was the head counselor. The staff made the decisions.

Focus

We consciously determined to work with what

we *could* change. We determined that we did not need to work more—that was hardly possible. We did need to work smarter, however. We could not fit any more into our time (we could not work any faster!), so we needed to reorganize a finite resource.

Communication

"Total" communication was the route we chose. The Restructuring Committee surveyed parents, students, and staff. Parents and students joined the committee on visitations and in decision making. The committee shared research, data, and models on a daily basis, in staff meetings, and in department meetings. The committee constantly solicited reactions and feedback from the staff, the school accountability

committee, and the community via weekly printed updates, newsletters, and before-school sessions.

From September of 1989 until February of 1990, the committee gathered input from educational research, professional articles, the National Education Association, the Colorado Department of Education, the University of Northern Colorado Lab School, existing schedules from throughout the nation (notably Pagosa Springs, Colorado), and surveys. Staff teams, often with parent and student partic-

ipation, made visitations to promising programs. We questioned, debated, and requestioned every issue. The staff had input at every step.

The committee generated alternatives, used various problem-solving strategies, and arrived at the Wasson Block Schedule—a change that was both structural and internalized, a change that was based on a philosophical re-evaluation among the staff, a change that would lead to and demand further changes. The staff voted in February of 1990 and approved the new schedule by 94 percent.

The change process was open, intense, thorough, and research-based.

Product

The Wasson Block Schedule consists of four 90-minute periods of instruction per day. There are

The change process was open, intense, thorough, and research-based.

15-minute passing periods between the first two blocks and between the last two blocks. Students and staff share a 50-minute lunch after the first two blocks. Two-semester classes under a traditional system (180 meetings of 50 minutes) are combined into a semester, or two terms (90 meetings of 90 minutes), and one-semester classes

under a traditional system (90 meetings of 50 minutes) are combined into a quarter, or one term (45 meetings of 90 minutes). Advanced Placement classes meet for three terms. The year consists of four terms, and if a student takes four courses each term, he or she can earn 16 credits a year. Sophomores and juniors, unless a reduced load is arranged with the administration, take four classes each term. Seniors must take a minimum of three. Most clubs and organizations meet during the 50-minute lunch break, as do many departments and committees.

Rewards (Results)

The 1990-91 school year marked the inception of the Wasson Block Schedule, and we are still on that schedule with only

minor changes. We are very pleased with the results and would not return to our previous schedule. Here's why:

1. The day is much less frantic. Students and teachers have time to move calmly from class to class. Student conflicts in the halls have decreased because there are fewer passing times and because the need to run no longer exists. Teachers can keep a student after class for five or 10 minutes to discuss a problem or make-up work, and the student can still be on time to his or her next class.

Lunch time is no longer a dangerous car race to the nearest fast food or a rushed in-building bite. More students are involved in clubs and organizations

because meetings take place during the lunch break when bus students can participate. Make-up work can be scheduled during this time also, as can most department meetings.

At any one time, teachers have fewer students (3 blocks x 30 students = 90 students), and students have fewer classes, so there are fewer interpersonal (and so higher quality) contacts and less record keeping per day and per week. Teachers take attendance only 15 times a week instead of 25 times.

Office messages for students, homework collection, settling in at the beginning of class and restlessness at the end, getting out and putting away materials, and all other such distractions happen about half as often. The faculty's

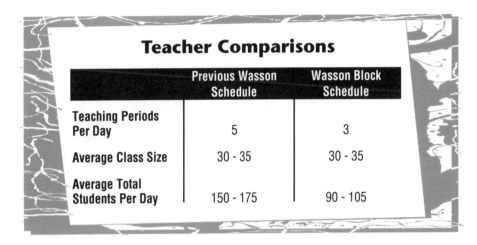

Teacher Comparisons

	Previous Wasson Schedule	Wasson Block Schedule
Teaching Periods Per Day	5	3
Average Class Size	30 - 35	30 - 35
Average Total Students Per Day	150 - 175	90 - 105

focus and energy are on three, not five classes; the students' focus and energy are on four, not five, six, or seven classes.

2. Students can earn more credits each year. On the traditional schedule of seven periods a day, students could earn a maximum of 14 credits per year. Now it is possible to earn 16. For some students this means early graduation is possible, but the faculty's philosophy is that students can now take more varied courses (i.e., "fit in" music as well as art) or elect to take more time to finish a particular course (i.e., complete Algebra I in three terms instead of two—still receiving only two credits).

Our students and parents share our philosophy. The early graduation

option has only been slightly more popular than it was on the traditional schedule, and our elective programs have expanded—more offerings, more students in those courses.

3. Each teacher has one full 90-minute block as a planning period. The block of time, as opposed to slightly more time split into two periods, allows for extremely productive work. And because approximately one-fourth of the faculty, instead of one-seventh on the traditional schedule, has a common planning time, we have seen an increase in the number of interdisciplinary, team-taught courses. It is also easier to find time within the day to share and to meet to take our next restructuring steps.

4. The blocks give teachers and students opportunities to increase the quality of education. Lab classes have enough time to finish the activity. Some field trips can be completed in the class period, and, if not, at least students do not miss as many classes—rarely more than one other. Because students can get there and back within one block, teachers are incorporating more short, out-of-the-building experiences (to nearby parks, senior citizens' centers, elementary schools, etc.). For the same reasons, we find that community and business

guest presenters are better able to schedule one block on one day, rather than two periods on two days. One of our new electives involves an intense shadowing in various careers. Students can do this for half a day and still take two other courses.

5. More individualization is possible. As mentioned earlier, students have the opportunity to take more courses. For some, however, this has translated into being able to take a term or two longer to finish a particular course and still have the credits necessary to graduate. Individual learning rates can be more easily accommodated. The same is true for students who wish to move faster. Also, students who fail classes have more credits "to spend" retaking a class during the regular school

Faculty feared that perhaps today's students thrive on sound bytes and rapid flashes of information and so would not tolerate long, more in-depth periods of learning.

year, rather than paying for summer school.

6. The greatest advantage has been the faculty's control of the learn-ing time. We now engage in less fragmented instruction. Gone are the days of long lecture presentations with all practice given as homework. Teachers now present in a variety of ways, allow time for individual- and group-guided practice, and then give application and evaluation activities as homework. Our teaching methods have expanded, and student successes have increased.

Teachers have the time within one block to present material and concepts in ways compatible with all learning styles. We are using more team teaching, more cooperative learning, more hands-on and discovery activities.

The number of *F*s has dropped, but that has not been a result of lowered standards as evidenced by the fact that the number

of *A*s has not increased proportionately.

Students as well as teachers feel more focused, and the learning is clearly more in-depth. At first, faculty feared that perhaps today's students thrive on sound bytes and rapid flashes of information and so would not tolerate long, more in-depth periods of learning. What we have discovered, though, is that students for the most part hunger for exploration, for more than the surface, and for significant contact with adults. Longer periods of learning acknowledged these needs.

Summation

Have we solved all our problems? Have we reached the Promised Land? Decidedly not! While attendance and drop-out rates and grade-point averages have improved, we still have nonattenders and students who choose to remain disengaged from the learning process. We still have student-student and student-teacher conflicts. In addition, the block schedule has been especially difficult for courses such as band, choir, yearbook, and newspaper that need the same students all year.

Nevertheless, in spite of the problems, we would not return to the traditional schedule. For us, the benefits far outweigh the disadvantages. Because we so believe in the Wasson Block Schedule, we are working on realignments and fine-tunings to eliminate as many problems as possible.

Having had and believing in this success, the Wasson staff has begun the next major step—rein-visioning our curriculum. In October of 1993, Restructuring II was born. This committee intends to follow the same change model for this most arduous and far-reaching task, and we are fully confident that by using this process, our experienced, dedicated, and creative staff will design a curriculum that will prepare our students for the twenty-first century—and beyond!

One Last Note

In the fall of 1993, Wasson became a four-year high school, as did all other high schools in our district. The decision was made in late April, and school began in mid-August. In spite of very little time for preparation for such a shift, Wasson decided to integrate the ninth graders into the block schedule. To add to this challenge, we were not allowed to alter the districtwide ninth grade curriculum.

Again, in spite of problems, we are finding most of the students benefit from our schedule. Now all freshmen, sopho-mores, and juniors must be in four blocks each term. Obviously, the total number of credits that it is possible for a student to earn has increased.

Also, we began the year with 95-minute blocks and shorter passing periods to accommodate the 20 instructional days our school board cut from the 1993-94 school calendar. Within a month, however, we were able to reinstate the Wasson Block Schedule as described here — for all of the reasons enumerated here. This expe-rience has served to rein-force our commitment to this schedule.

While we could not go any faster, we could go differently, and we are glad that we did! ◆

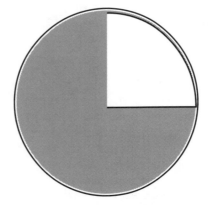

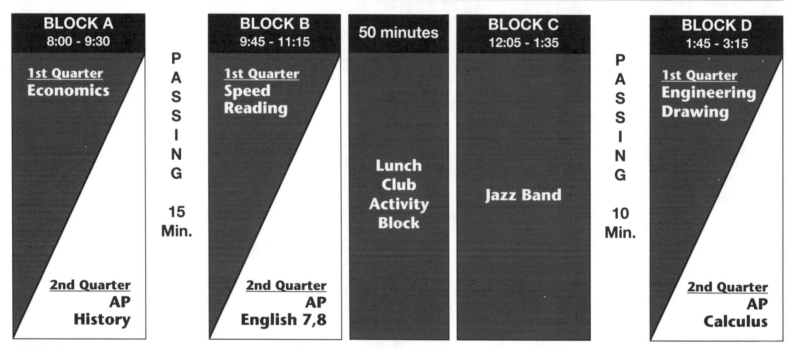

WASSON BLOCK SCHEDULE
TERMS 1 AND 2

BLOCK A
8:00 - 9:30

1st Quarter
Economics

2nd Quarter
**AP
History**

P
A
S
S
I
N
G

15
Min.

BLOCK B
9:45 - 11:15

1st Quarter
**Speed
Reading**

2nd Quarter
**AP
English 7,8**

50 minutes

**Lunch
Club
Activity
Block**

BLOCK C
12:05 - 1:35

Jazz Band

P
A
S
S
I
N
G

10
Min.

BLOCK D
1:45 - 3:15

1st Quarter
**Engineering
Drawing**

2nd Quarter
**AP
Calculus**

NOTE: This is not an example of a typical schedule. This attachment is used to illustrate features of the block plan.

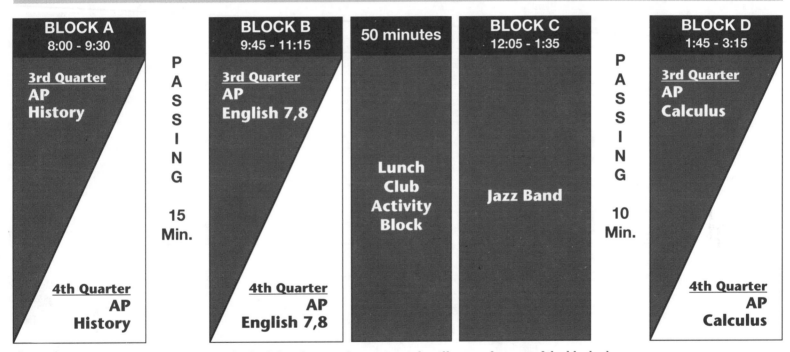

WASSON BLOCK SCHEDULE
TERMS 3 AND 4

BLOCK A
8:00 - 9:30

3rd Quarter
AP
History

4th Quarter
AP
History

PASSING 15 Min.

BLOCK B
9:45 - 11:15

3rd Quarter
AP
English 7,8

4th Quarter
AP
English 7,8

50 minutes

Lunch
Club
Activity
Block

BLOCK C
12:05 - 1:35

Jazz Band

PASSING 10 Min.

BLOCK D
1:45 - 3:15

3rd Quarter
AP
Calculus

4th Quarter
AP
Calculus

NOTE: This is not an example of a typical schedule. This attachment is used to illustrate features of the block plan.

Reader Reflections

Insights: _____

_____

_____

_____

_____

Actions for Our School (District) to Consider: _____

_____

_____

_____

_____

_____

_____

_____

*What the faculty discovered is that students
for the most part hunger for exploration, for more than the
surface, and for significant contact with adults.
Longer periods of learning acknowledged these needs.*

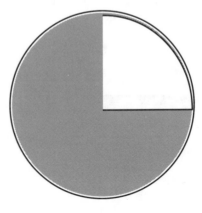

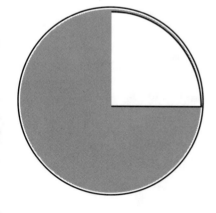

NEW KIDS ON THE BLOCK

Here's how we adapted the successful Wasson Block Plan to meet the specific needs of our students.

After 21 years in the military service and a couple of administrative jobs in the private sector, I fulfilled a lifetime dream of entering a high school classroom as "teacher." One of the first things I discovered when I finally got there was a serious lack of time. In all my previous work life, no matter how harried, nothing compared to the extreme shortage of available time I found in teaching. My colleagues share this complaint of "never enough time." In fact,

of all the educational resources in short supply—money, materials, equipment, and time—time is by far the resource we consider most in demand.

When I first began to ponder this issue, it struck me that we can increase or decrease all the other resources—money, materials, and equipment— but the clock and calendar are pretty well fixed. We cannot add

more days to the calendar, nor minutes in a day. Whatever power we gain over the clock or calendar, then, is in the way we use the time allotted us.

Archaic Views Of Time

Unfortunately, we have seen little change in the way we schedule this allotted time since the beginning of public education in America. We con-

tinue to base our school calendar on an agrarian society that, to be quite honest, no longer exists. Farm kids are not the farm laborers they once were. Machinery has largely replaced the demands on students as part-time producers of food. However, such changes in technology and social structure have not altered our archaic use of the farm year as a standard for our school calendar.

What seems even more out of tune with our times is the use of the clock. We still operate our school

JAY C. PIERSON

Integrated Learning Specialist
William B. Travis High School
Austin, Texas

day according to a factory production model not unlike that designed by Frederick Taylor, an early efficiency expert, who was highly respected in the days when human beings were considered little more than an extension of machines.

Yet today, little work is performed by a lone, assembly-line worker. Worker interactions, team planning, and group problem solving have become more

... the clock and calendar are pretty well fixed. We cannot add more days to the calendar, nor minutes in a day.

and more the norm.

Our schools, however, still operate as though the student were an empty, inanimate vessel, subjected to a 12-year filling-up process, accomplished in individual rooms, by individual dispensers (teachers), not unlike a turn-of-the-century manufacturing process. We ring a bell every 50 minutes and send our "vessels" off to another station to assure that the assembly line is moving at the appropriate pace.

We may be moving students promptly from room to room, but we are not educating them adequately. Today, we face an incredibly high dropout rate. According to the U.S. Department of Education, one in four of our entering freshmen will not graduate. The results of an antiquated system don't stop there: We retain a large number of our freshman students because they are unable to keep up with the academic requirements in their first-year transition to the demands of high school. We have a high number of failures. Even those students who graduate often fall short of possessing the necessary skills for the next stage of life, whether it be the workplace or higher education.

I believe educators are working as hard and as many hours as possible. (That's why teaching ranks near the top on every list of high-stress professions.) The way I see it, it's not a question of working harder, but of working differently.

Currently, most teachers (particularly high school teachers) feel pressed to accomplish the impossible in 50-minute time frames, while their students often see the small segments of instruction as unrelated fragments. There seems to be little or no continuity between what students learn from one class to the next. And, in the process we sort students, graduate the survivors, and let the rest drop through the cracks.

It has been said that if Rip Van Winkle awoke today, the one modern institution he would recognize is the school. It has changed little in 200 years.

We do not just need restructuring or revolution. We need total reculturing. And, we had better move fast, or we may well produce a generation of Rip Van Winkles who will sleep though 12 years of "education" and wake up in a still familiar place. The worst part is, these students will probably still qualify for whatever diploma we offer.

Responding to The Times

After 12 years of teaching in an inner-city school and watching the population change from one that equitably reflected the ethnic and socioeconomic makeup of the community, to one with a large low socioeconomic student body, I came to realize that schooling had changed dramatically whether we were ready to acknowledge it or not. The traditional methods of teaching were archaic for students who did not possess a great deal of parental involvement in their learning or a rich background of experiences. Many of our students were either from single-parent, or two working-parent households where little time goes for reading and interaction between parent and child. Most of what my students knew best, came from too many hours of viewing television, and much of what they watched had little bearing on the realities of the world in which they were teenagers.

The Birth of IMAGE

I remember clearly an afternoon about six years ago, as these demographic changes were beginning to affect our school population, a group of us (our principal and several teachers) were enjoying coffee and cake, in celebration of a coach's birthday. We began to discuss our kids and the changed world into which they would enter upon graduation. We fully understood that our students were not prepared for the world they faced. We began to consider the need for a meaningful curriculum of global education and interdisciplinary studies.

Out of that "coffee break" discussion came the impetus for what we now call IMAGE, (International, Multicultural, and Global Education). As part of those first efforts to rethink the way we educate our students, we associated ourselves with NEA's Mastery in Learning Consortium (MILC), a group of schools that work together to develop teacher-initiated school improvement. Being an MILC school helped us to connect with several other schools throughout the country that were facing up to current problems and trying to find solutions. We began with them what will undoubtedly be a long journey.

The Trip to Wasson High

As a part of that MILC involvement, a group of us, including our principal, Ms. Elena Vela, attended a conference in Colorado Springs, Colorado. There we participated in various

---

How Would Student Contact And Teacher Preparation Change?

We did some calculating to determine how student contact and teacher preparation time would change if we moved to 90-minute block scheduling. According to our calculations, in the course of one semester, teacher/student contact time would increase by 30 hours (60 hours over one year), and teacher planning time would nearly double.

Period Length	Number Periods	Number Days	Contact Hours	Total Hours	Planning Days
50 minutes	Five	90	375	75	9.375
90 minutes	Three	90	405	135	16.875

seminars on restructuring and related issues. I reluctantly signed up for a visit to Wasson High, a local school where the teachers had adopted a different time structure for their school day. A colleague, Janice Hensley, also attended the Wasson presentation.

Wasson had developed a block schedule suitable to its needs. Instead of six 50-minute periods per day as we at Travis High

Whatever power we gain over the clock or calendar, then, is in the way we use the time we are allotted.

School were using, the Wasson school had opted for four 90-minute periods per day. The principal, Mr. Houston, and members of his staff explained the rationale and process of adopting such a system and discussed all they had done to make it work.

I began to realize that they had, in fact, designed a system that might just add power to what we were trying to do in Austin, Texas. As I purposefully wandered around the Wasson campus, talking to teachers and students, I became more and more convinced that the block schedule was an option we should at least consider. My colleague Janice Hensley had a similar positive response to what she had seen and heard.

Fortunately, we at Travis High School have a principal who encourages innovation and teacher-led change. As we flew back from Colorado, Janice and I talked with Ms. Vela at some length about the possibilities of instituting the block plan for Travis. Ms. Vela made a number of suggestions for refinements, based on Texas and Austin Independent School District requirements and the needs of our kids. We immediately began to outline a workable plan to present the block concept to the faculty and staff. By the time we de-planed in Austin, we felt we had developed an exciting proposal for bringing about significant change in the way our students progress through high school.

Those of us who had made the Colorado Springs trip knew if our school adopted such a plan, the change would be difficult. We would all have to change the way we taught school. And, the way we taught was exactly the way we had experienced school through more than 16 years of formal education. It was the only way we knew how to teach. We had experienced 50-minute sound and sight bytes in education for our entire lives and now we were considering not only an entirely new clock schedule, but more importantly, an entirely new way for our students to participate in their own learning.

Changing to Block Scheduling

We spent many hours in active discussion over switching to the block plan. We gathered in various locations and at various times (during lunch, before school, and after school), airing our concerns and the pros and cons of the plan. At the conclusion of those exchanges, we adopted a number of beliefs that guided our process. They are:

• Students will take up to four courses instead of the present six. At least two of those should be core academic courses, while the other two will likely be athletics and an elective class. This will allow students to more thoroughly prepare for each class without sacrificing studies in another. They will have fewer materials and assignments to manage.

• Students can gain more credits during their high school years. The four-block schedule will allow (eight credits) per year, compared to the present (six credits). Thus, in a four-year period a student could accumulate as many as 32 credits, compared to the present maximum of 24.

• The expanded (90-minute vs. 50-minute) periods will allow students to experience learning situations that will expose them to a variety of teaching and teaming methods.

• The opportunity for re-enrollment in previously failed courses during the same academic year will allow students to achieve the appropriate number of credits required to be at grade level for the next academic year. Because dropout rates closely correlate with being behind grade level, this opportunity can have considerable impact.

• Student stress will decrease substantially. Focusing on four classes, rather than six, will allow students to participate in extracurricular activities, family activities, and part-time employment while still experiencing academic success.

• Students who individually and collectively experience academic success, tend to have a greater ownership of their school, and so will become more involved in all facets of the school community.

In addition to our developed beliefs concerning students, we adopted the following concepts concerning curriculum and instructional methods:

• Such a schedule will allow for changes in instructional methods that will meet the needs of students with varied learning styles.

• Teachers will have opportunities to develop lessons based on varied instructional techniques.

• They will rely less on lecture and more on critical thinking, problem solving, cooperative teaming, and interdisciplinary projects.

• The block schedule will provide greater opportunity for completion of lab projects.

• Setting up and breaking down labs would need to

...it's not a question of working harder, but of working differently.

be done only once in a 90-minute block, whereas it is now done twice during that same time in two 50-minute class periods.

• Opportunities for team teaching and increased planning time will allow teachers to jointly plan, prepare, and teach courses (environmental science and geography, for example).

• There will be more opportunities for use of community resources (guest speakers and field trips) and formation of partnerships with the business and academic communities.

One of our major concerns was how the change in schedule would impact teacher-student planning time. The chart on page 53

...most...high school teachers feel pressed to accomplish the impossible in 50-minute time frames, while their students often see the small segments of instruction as unrelated fragments.

gives a brief synopsis of those calculations.

According to these calculations, in the course of one semester, teacher-student contact time would increase by 30 hours (60 hours during one year). Teacher planning time would nearly double.

The general consensus among those members of the staff who took time from their busy schedule to seek information about this issue was very positive. In a straw poll, we found the overwhelming majority of the Travis faculty to be in support of the block plan (more than 80% responded positively).

Several teachers involved their students in a discussion of the plan and sought feedback. Following are a few of the questions we asked students, and the responses they gave.

Question: What do you like about this schedule?
Responses:
• opportunity to earn more credits
• time to take more electives
• time to take more core/college prep courses
• time to take a failed class over
• fewer classes per semester
• longer class periods
• time to breathe during class
• more time to absorb the material
• more time to work with other students
• greater teacher/student interaction.

Question: What do you dislike about this schedule?

Responses:
• long class time with no break
• shorter lunch period.

Question: What classes would you like to take that are also now offered at Travis High School?
Responses:
• art (drawing, comic art, design, commercial art, printing)
• business (advertising, personal finance, management)
• languages (sign, Japanese, Portuguese)
• P.E. (bowling, boxing, Hispanic dance)
• cosmetology (on this campus) and modeling
• basic law and law enforcement
• courses about medicine or nursing
• study hall and tutoring courses.

Question: Would you like

Travis High School to implement this type of schedule next fall?

Responses:
Yes—84%
No—8%
Undecided—4%
Unconcerned ("I don't care.")— 8%.

Implementing And Refining The Block Plan

At the conclusion of the 1990-91 school year, the decision was made to begin the next school year under the block plan. A number of our teachers worked throughout the summer to reschedule students who had previously been scheduled under the old system and to form interdisciplinary teams of teachers and students for the incoming freshman class. Scheduling was a difficult task, but we immediately confronted and resolved all problems.

When the 1992-93 school year began, William B. Travis High School was on the block schedule.

Now in our second year, we discuss the change as successful. Teachers have performed beyond the call of duty to make it work. Staff development has taken on a new meaning as educators have endeavored to learn new ways to teach that make use of the newest research in education. Due to this change and other IMPACT actions, our curriculum is in an ongoing process of revision. Cooperative learning and authentic assessment have become the keys to our success. We are still learning how to make these important changes and will continue to learn from and share our experiences. We have learned that educational reform is not simply restructuring.

We have learned that educational reform is not simply restructuring. It is, in fact, reculturing.

It is, in fact, reculturing. As we grow and evaluate this process, nearly all of us would agree that although the process has been difficult as well as rewarding, none of us would go back to the way it was. ◆

Breakdown of the School Year
Travis High School, Austin, Texas

Old Schedule	Block Schedule
One year = two 18-week semesters	One year = two 18-week semesters
One semester = three six-week grade periods	One semester = three six-week grade periods
Six classes per semester	Four classes per semester
Three credits per semester	Four credits per semester
Six credits per school year	Eight credits per school year
24 credits in four years	32 credits in four years

Breakdown of the School Day
Travis High School, Austin, Texas

Old School Day	Block School Day
Six 50-minute classes	Four 90-minute classes
Four three-minute passing periods	Two 10 minute passing periods
55- to 70-minute lunch	50-minute lunch
25-minute activity period	30-minute activity period
Teacher Load - Five classes 100- 150 students	Teacher Load - Three classes 50-70 students
Student Load - Six classes Four to five academic core	Student Load - Four classes Two to three academic core

Characteristics of a Learning-Centered Schedule

① **The schedule maximizes instructional time.** The schedule reflects curricular priorities and gives first priority to students' learning needs. Administrators and teachers cooperate in defending instructional time.

② **The schedule facilitates the professional growth of teachers.** Teachers have time to plan collaboratively and to cooperate in fostering their professional growth.

③ **The schedule reflects grouping practices that do not stigmatize students.** It gives all students access to a quality curriculum and fosters student achievement.

④ **The schedule gives teachers a teachable situation.** Teachers are assigned to their area of specialization. Wherever possible, teacher preferences about the number and type of preparations and room assignments are acknowledged. Classes are neither too large nor excessively heterogeneous.

⑤ **The schedule is flexible and learning-oriented.** Time is organized according to learning needs, instead of learning being constrained by rigid time frameworks.

⑥ **The schedule is responsive to the needs of students and teachers.** Sufficient time is provided for relaxing, eating, and taking care of personal needs.

Source: From *Teachers As Agents of Change,* by Allan A. Glatthorn, Washington, D.C., National Education Association, 1992. Based on research by Anderson 1984, Dempsey and Traverso 1983, and Glatthorn 1986.

Reader Reflections

Insights: _____

_____

_____

_____

_____

Actions for Our School (District) to Consider: _____

_____

_____

_____

_____

_____

_____

_____

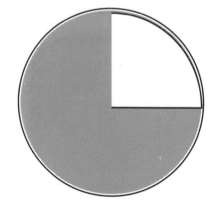

THE PARKLAND PROJECT

We established a plan up-front for fostering student, community, and administrative buy-in to our new school schedule.

It was January of 1992, and our Parkland High School staff in Winston-Salem, North Carolina, was beginning to unravel because we could not agree on a project for school restructuring. As one of six sites in the National Education Association's Mastery-in-Learning Consortium Project (an education reform initiative), we felt pressured to undertake a new look at the high school structure. So far, we had only succeeded in creating more territorial strife among staff members.

We on the School Improvement Team met for hours each week trying to define a major focus for our project. We had discussed and tabled adopting a year-round school schedule because the community had not seemed ready for this vast change. We were instrumental in encouraging technology mini-projects and interdisciplinary approaches to classroom instruction, but these were departmentalized and did not affect all members of the staff—a goal we had set so that every student, parent, teacher, support person, and administrator could share in the impact of our restructuring efforts. We were well into the second year of our commitment to a large-scale project and still had not secured a plan.

During a staff development day in January, two teachers—Karen Oxendine and Nora Baker—presented a session on alternative scheduling methods for the high school day. Nora presented the Copernican Plan and another similar modular possibility, while Karen shared the plan she had discovered in Colorado Springs at the NEA Symposium in November 1991—the block schedule implemented by Colorado's Wasson High School. In this schedule, students take four courses in extended class periods

SANDY TREADWAY

Guidance Counselor

Parkland High School

Winston-Salem, North Carolina

for half of the school year.

By the end of the session, the staff began to discuss changing our traditional six-period day. In the days that followed, teachers discussed the possibilities further in the lounge, on lunch duty, and at coffee gatherings. The block schedule soon emerged as the schedule choice, and implementing this schedule looked like a good Mastery-in-Learn-

A block schedule suddenly began to look like the most promising method to meet the needs of everyone.

ing Consortium (MILC) project for us. It became the one proposal that appeared to benefit the students and teachers while also addressing the needs of the community.

Parkland High School Community

To give you a better idea of those needs, let me tell you a little bit about our community. Parkland High School is on the south side of Winston-Salem, a mid-sized community of approximately 150,000 people. Parkland serves 1,100 students in grades nine through 12. It is the senior high component of an MILC site that includes two feeder schools: Konnoak Elementary School and Philo Middle School. Most schools in the Winston-Salem/Forsyth County School System depend upon busing to achieve racial balance, but our three schools have naturally integrated school populations. You could say we are about the only "neighborhood" schools left in the city.

While neighborhoods are racially mixed, most members are primarily lower and middle class blue-collar workers where many of the parents either attended Parkland High School or one of the older high schools that merged to create Parkland. Consequently, many community members take a very keen interest in the school's progress and daily events long after their children have left the school.

Although education beyond high school has not been a top priority in the minds of these parents, they instill a strong work ethic in their children, and they want them to earn a high school diploma.

Our 1992 staff had higher expectations for its students and so was faced with the prospect of delivering more academic, technical, and aesthetic opportunities within the time frame of a traditional high school day. Adding to this challenge, the state had increased academic graduation requirements, significantly narrowing elective choices for students on a traditional schedule. A block schedule suddenly began to look like the most promising method to meet the needs of everyone.

How to Exact The Change?

In March of 1992, the Parkland staff voted 86 percent in favor of the four-period day. Now, the real work was to begin. How could we inform the students, parents, and school system administrative staff of our intentions?

Because our focus is on

How Does Parkland's Schedule Work?

Each year, a student registers for eight courses. The schedule permits a student to take two or three academic courses and one or two elective courses each quarter. Below is an example of how the school year is divided and a sample of a student's course load.

August-January		January-June	
1st Quarter	**2nd Quarter**	**3rd Quarter**	**4th Quarter**
English I Algebra I P.E. Band I	English I Algebra I Health Band I	Social Studies Geometry French I Band II	Social Studies Geometry French I Band II
eight semester credits		eight semester credits	

Eight semester credits = four credits toward graduation. Within a year, a student could earn 16 semester credits (eight credits toward graduation).

our students, and we truly count them as the most important factor in our reason for restructuring, we wanted to present our plan to them first. It so happened that March is always the time the guidance counselors talk with students about course registration for the next school year. We decided that while conducting this orientation, the counselors could solicit students' input on the schedule change.

At Parkland, orientation for course selection occurs in class-sized groups of no more than 30 students so that everyone is comfortable enough to ask questions and to understand the opportunities available for the next year. It was during these 50-minute presentations that the counselors presented the idea of taking four courses at a time for 90-minute sessions for half of the school year, and then taking four different courses for the remainder of the year to increase the number of possible credits to eight per school year.

While students voiced apprehension over the extended class periods, they quickly embraced the chance to take higher academic levels, more than one foreign language, more art and music, and vocational/technical courses that they had not previously had time to include in their plans. After a few sessions, word traveled around the school, and the counselors no longer had to explain the schedule, but to listen to the students' enthusiasm and try to answer their questions about what they could do to speed the adoption of the new schedule.

After orientation, the counselors then register each student individually for next year. During this registration, they asked every student what the change would mean to him or her personally. In addition, these personal sessions gave the counselors the chance to tell each student about the upcoming meeting to introduce the plan to the community and to encourage each student to bring a parent with him or her to the gathering. We also mailed notices to all of our students and to the current eighth graders as well.

Taking It to the Community

In April of 1992, we conducted this "town meeting" to involve our parents (and students further) in our proposed change. We began with a large gathering in the auditorium to outline the basic structure of the block schedule, but quickly moved to pairing teachers with small groups of 10 to 15 students and parents so that we could answer questions and share our feelings about the change. In addition, we listened carefully to concerns and strong feelings about students' not taking English, math, or foreign language for an entire year. We, too, had reservations about these changes, but we felt the risk was worth implementing.

change our schedule. Our next step was to take our findings and our plan to our school superintendent, Larry Coble, and his administrative team.

Convincing the Power Sources

After our community meeting, the faculty was so excited about the prospect of changing that we had to narrow the delegation that would present our ideas to the superintendent and his staff to 15 faculty members. Armed with statistics of the students' course selec-

tions, their comments, and their parents' support, we pleaded with the administrative team to allow us to begin the new schedule in the 1992-93 school year.

While the administrative team worried about additional costs of implementation, the lack of time to provide staff development, and the computer knowledge necessary to create a workable master schedule, the Parkland staff challenged and answered every hesitation with powerful conviction. We asked for no additional staff and no additional funding. As an MILC site, we had been exposed to more extensive staff development training than our colleagues at other local high schools and believed we could handle the change. Finally, we were so energized with

this change that many staff members planned to give up precious summer vacation to help create the new schedule.

Despite many of the administrative team's reservations about our being able to make this schedule change by the beginning of the school year in August, Dr. Coble and his staff granted their permission the first week in June. We had won, but the work was just beginning.

The Block Schedule: Merely Framework

Although the Parkland staff viewed the schedule as the best means to educate our students, we knew that this time change was no more than a structure. What we did within the time frame would determine the success of our project. Conse-

...we knew that this time change was no more than a structure. What we did within the time frame would determine the success of our project.

Finally, at the conclusion of the community meeting, we took a "straw" vote, and the parents supported our proposal to

quently, at the core of our restructuring efforts was the staff's commitment to vary teaching strategies and to address students' various learning styles within each class period.

Our curriculum coordinator, Cathy Stankwytch, who had been organizing our staff development schedule for the last two years, carefully planned power-packed sessions for the August workdays to help everyone adjust to the longer class times. Knowing that our staff was suspicious of "experts who were no longer in the trenches," Cathy coerced staff members to teach sessions in their areas of creativity.

During these workdays, every staff member—including administrators and support personnel—attended sessions on cooperative learning, cognitive mapping, technology in the classroom, seminar teaching, academic games, and student centers. Using Parkland staff members had a two-fold purpose: to prove that these methods were already being used effectively at the school by "regular" teachers and to provide a source within the building to help perfect and refine the techniques that were being shared. By having "in-house experts," those teachers who had some difficulties in changing their teaching styles from the traditional lecture method needed only to travel down the hall to get some help in varying their techniques.

Although the staff members vowed to alter their teaching styles, this portion of the schedule change has been the most difficult and challenging problem to address. In the 1992-93 school year, both veteran and new teachers shared the burden of how to address their coursework within a new time frame. Planning, condensing, and determining key elements of the courses took more time and more patience for trial-and-error strategies than teachers had expected. Each

Timetable for Fostering Student, Community, and Administrative Buy-In

Here's how we got students, parents, and school system administrators positively involved in our plan to switch to block scheduling.

MARCH
•Our guidance counselors solicited students' input on the schedule change during the annual orientation meetings they conduct to help students plan their schedules for the coming year. (Each meeting consists of approximately 30 students.)

•Guidance counselors spoke to each student individually about the plan as he or she officially registered for next year's courses.

APRIL
•Staff members conducted a town meeting for students and parents. We began with a large gathering in the auditorium to outline the basic structure of the block schedule, but quickly moved to pairing teachers with small groups of 10 to15 students and parents so that we could answer questions and share our feelings about the change.

MAY
•A delegation of 15 faculty members presented our case to the school superintendent and his administrative staff. Armed with statistics of the students' course selections, their comments, and their parents' support, we pleaded with the administrative team to allow us to begin the new schedule in the 1992-93 school year.

The first week in June, school system administrators gave the OK!

department established pacing guides for each course, and these guides are in a constant flux as teachers are still working to refine their course studies. However, despite the increased workloads, the faculty has become closer and more convinced that this time frame is better for our students.

Because teachers are

subject matter. Writing across the curriculum has become a reality and is no longer the English teachers' sole responsibility, as students have only half of the school year in language arts. In spending 90 minutes a day with each class, teachers also have a better opportunity to connect with each student during the

it does not happen by chance, and it is not achieved without problems and surprises. The key element is ownership, with the shareholders/teachers creating the atmosphere and defining the framework. While administrative support is essential to success, the teachers must be the power force of design if the change is to be effective.

At Parkland, the staff instituted the change and established the parameters for development. We realized just how much we had created this plan and had accepted full responsibility for its implementation when our superintendent assigned us a new principal and three new assistant principals in July, just one month before we began the block schedule!

Because our new high school administrative

team members had not been at Parkland during the planning stages, we had to convince them that what we were doing had merit, and we had to instruct them in how it would work. Our new principal, James Brandon, placed his faith in the staff and organized his administrative team to provide the necessary discipline and support to enhance our efforts.

As a result of this collaboration, Parkland High School completed its first year under the block schedule and is in the midst of a second, more settled school year. Although our overall North Carolina End-of-Course Test scores were lower than the previous year, we improved in June from our January results and anticipate more improvement this year. Our reten-

...at the core of our restructuring efforts was the staff's commitment to vary teaching strategies and to address students' various learning styles within each class period.

working with only approximately 70 students at a time, they are able to assign more research projects and offer more in-depth approaches to their

period, allowing natural advocacy to occur.

Conclusion

While change is both exhilarating and frightening,

tion rates for students earning more than five units per school year improved by six percent, with our ninth graders increasing by 10 percent. We also experienced an eight percent increase in seniors who qualified for admission into the University of North Carolina system—a greater gain than any of the other high schools in our system.

On a more subjective note, the students and staff report that the block schedule provides a calmer, less stressful school day. Because students have only three "passing periods" between classes, our discipline problems have been significantly reduced. With the rapid pace established in classes to cover the subject matter, students and teachers realize that time is our most precious commodity. Consequently, the halls are empty during class time because students are actively involved in their courses.

From the staff perspective, teacher attendance has greatly improved. Burnout does not occur because teachers are working with fewer students; they have fewer class preparations; and they have longer planning sessions. This renewal has fostered more faculty social events and has created a bonding of a staff that had previously seemed destined to form strong splinter groups of dissension.

Parkland is gaining respect in the community and throughout the state as an innovative high school. While we may never be the school of choice in Winston-Salem, we are gaining a newfound appreciation in the city, and our students are strutting their "Parkland Pride" as they receive recognition for our unique approach.

To date, we have entertained more than 500 visitors and have allowed them to enter any of our classes to view firsthand how we structure the 90-minute periods. Because we fervently believe that the time schedule is only the structure and that the diverse teaching strategies are the true force of change, we are eager to share our successes and provide assistance for avoiding some of the pitfalls. Parkland High School is in the business for students, and it is this focus that defines our main impetus for restructuring. ◆

Planning, condensing, and determining key elements of the courses took more time and more patience for trial-and-error strategies than teachers had expected.

So You Want to Implement a Block Schedule...

Staff members at Parkland High School in Winston-Salem, North Carolina,
recommend you consider the following:

1 With block scheduling, your lower-ability students only have to concentrate on four subjects at a time, providing them more time to master the coursework and allowing them more academic success.

2 With block scheduling, your higher-ability students are able to upgrade their academic subjects while being able to take advantage of performing arts and/or vocational subjects that have previously been unavailable in a traditional time frame.

3 With students earning credits more rapidly, you may need to adopt or revise an early graduation policy. So far, Parkland High School has not encountered problems in this area. Because we emphasize the increased opportunities for future preparation, dual enrollment with local colleges, and enrichment at no extra charge, we have not had many students seek early graduation. Those who do request it must have a written plan to present to the principal by August of their senior year so that they may finish their coursework by January. Because we do not allow a student to take English IV until the fourth year, no one is eligible for graduation earlier than January of the fourth year.

4 Staff development and commitment to changing teaching styles are the two most important factors for success of the block schedule. It may take two years or paid vacation periods to offer teachers in your school enough training to be effective.

5 If your school system is tied to Carnegie units, you may have to apply to the state to allow you more flexible class time.

So You Want to Implement a Block Schedule…(continued)

6 In creating the master schedule, your staff must decide whether a student can repeat a failed course immediately or must wait until the next school year. This consideration may also determine whether you schedule students for the entire year, or if you need to devise two master schedules for the school year.

7 Before implementing your block schedule, you must decide how often students will receive report cards, when to administer exams, and how attendance will affect outcomes. Because courses move more rapidly, absence from class is a serious problem. How students can make up work must be planned before implementation—after school programs, Saturday school, and summer school are some alternatives.

8 Transfer students from traditional high schools may present a challenge, depending upon what time of the year they enroll in your school. Students who transfer into your school or from your school always run the risk of losing credits, but for incoming students, the ability to earn up to eight units a year usually allows time to make up credits.

9 Writing can no longer be the domain of the English teacher. We believe in "writing across the curriculum" and more of the academic and elective courses are including research projects in their standard course of study. We also deliberately set up a relationship with English and social studies so that if a student has English the first half of any school year, he or she has social studies the second half. The same pairing often is established for science and math as well, so that most students have at least two academic requirements each half of the year.

10 While we anticipated higher enrollment in our vocational electives, we were surprised to find that many students chose upper levels of math, more foreign language, and additional courses in science and English. We did not gain any staff members, and so some of our academic class loads increased to 30 students. Many of our elective courses filled to capacity as well. As a result, some teachers may be teaching more students in a school year than the state maximum.

Reader Reflections

Insights: _____

_____

_____

_____

_____

Actions for Our School (District) to Consider: _____

_____

_____

_____

_____

_____

_____

_____

*The key element is ownership,
with the shareholders/teachers creating the atmosphere
and defining the framework.*

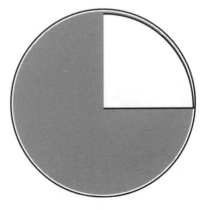

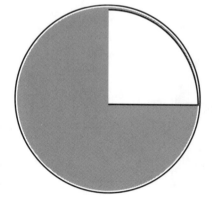

KEEPING PACE

Through careful collaboration, these educators reallocated school time in a way that allowed instruction to "keep up with the times."

You might say that we at North Eugene High School in Oregon are veterans of school change. We became involved in an ongoing restructuring effort more than seven years ago, when supported by several grants, we decided to explore futurist literature and to invite visionary speakers to address the staff. We also read the educational research regarding restructuring and visited schools around the country that were moving in promising new directions.

Not long after that, we consulted with David Conley of the University of Oregon, a noted authority on school restructuring, and as a result, adopted his Dimensions of Restructuring model, with its three central variables: (1) curriculum—what we teach, (2) instruction—how we teach, and (3) assessment—how we evaluate students.

JULIE TAYLOR, Spanish Teacher
KEVIN McCAULEY, Biology Teacher
BOB ANDERSON, Principal
North Eugene High School
Eugene, Oregon

These central variables all revolve around the centerpiece of learning, namely, student outcomes. This model helped us see the need to change our classrooms from teacher-centered to student-centered, and to recognize that our restructuring efforts must focus on curriculum, instruction, and assessment.

Conley's model also incorporates supporting variables including the use of time, but emphasizes that changing schedules should be the result of a conscious decision to improve curriculum, instruction, and assessment.

Viewing time as a variable also implies that students don't learn at the same rate, and this prompted us to examine our current use of seat time and Carnegie units as a yardstick of student success.

Then, too, work done by Theodore Sizer and his Coalition of Essential Schools questions the value of learning information on a vast number of topics in a time when information is growing exponentially. Sizer's notion of "less is more" (in-depth understanding of fewer topics) caused our staff to begin examining curricular content and its importance or relevance.

In addition to considering society in the future and exploring school restructuring research, we performed an extensive self-evaluation. Using *On-*

identifying our strong and weak points, (2) for using these points to plan school-improvement efforts, and (3) for making comparisons in future years.

Time for a Change

As we began to shift our measurement of student success from seat time and Carnegie units to portfolio demonstrations of performance standards, we noticed many shortcomings in our seven-period day. For example, from our re-

need to involve our students in more tasks that incorporated cooperative learning if we were to adequately prepare them for their roles as adult workers. The depth and quality of inquiry that a large-scale project affords also seemed to be a positive outcome for our students, and yet teachers felt their students were no sooner productively on task, when the 50-minute bell would ring, and off they'd go.

There were other shortcomings as well. Our new emphasis on encouraging students to be active learners, with teachers as "coaches" instead of "information givers," appeared to be hindered by the shorter periods. The frenetic pace of students going to seven different classes, and teachers trying to teach 150 plus students per day created a

harried atmosphere for both teachers and students alike, and relationships were harder to develop. In addition, the necessity to create larger classes in a time of diminishing resources seemed to intensify the hectic nature of the classrooms and hallways. It was increasingly apparent that something had to change.

The shared vision that had emerged from our staff's research prompted us to investigate a number of alternative school schedules. After attending conferences on daily schedules, networking with other schools involved in using time differently, reading the available research on longer periods, and visiting schools that have either implemented a four-period day or were preparing to do so, a group of us de-

...changing schedules should be the result of a conscious decision to improve curriculum, instruction, and assessment.

ward to Excellence, a data-based instrument for school evaluation, North staffers collected baseline information to use: (1) for

search we learned that people in the workplace are more often working collaboratively instead of in isolation. We saw a

ided to formally request that North High School adopt the four-period model in which students took either three or four 90-minute classes per 18 weeks, which would be the equivalent of year-long classes in the old model.

At North, staff members have a say in the way things are done, and decisions are not made at the top. In fact, we make major decisions through consensus, which causes less division among the staff, but takes more time. The steps we took to gain consensus on the four-period day included the following:

- We piloted blocks in some departments.
- We looked at existing models.
- We shared research with the entire staff.
- We shared our plans with students.
- We shared our plans with parents.
- Each department leader interviewed each member of his or her department to get input.
- We worked with the Eugene Education Association (the teachers' union) from the beginning to make sure that no contractual problems would arise.
- The administration worked with the AP students to determine scheduling frameworks with the fewest possible conflicts for them.
- The administration also worked with the teachers in special areas such as music, debate, and theater, to determine the best type of schedule for them.
- We kept our feeder schools and parents of incoming students informed of our intentions.

In the spring of last year, we reached consensus on changing to the four-period day. We agreed to commit to it for one year, after which time we would evaluate the program. The process was lengthy, but because we invested time and energy at the outset, we believe we reduced many problems that usually arise when change takes place.

Preparing for the Time Change

Many teachers were concerned about teaching longer lessons. They asked tough questions such as: How can we hold the students' interest for 90 minutes? How many new concepts can we introduce in the same day? Teachers also wondered if they would have to drop some course material in order to squeeze one year's worth

of study into an overall time frame that amounts to 15 fewer instructional hours. Together, we developed a number of strategies for teaching within the new framework. These were helpful, but after a few months of actual experience, we outlined the following, which are even more helpful.

1. Pacing is tricky at first! Plan long-term (with dates) to avoid having to increase pace during the last six weeks. Chances are you will not be able to compress twice as much into one 90-minute period as in two 50-minute periods, so examine curriculum carefully.

2. Provide a variety of activities to keep students

from tuning out. Try to incorporate different skills (reading, writing, listening, speaking) and different learning styles (hands-on, visual aids) within the same block.

3. Plan for movement within a lesson. Have students get out of their seats to pick up tests and other papers instead of handing them out; have them move into pairs or small groups; send them to the library.

4. Make use of peer tu-

Viewing time as a variable also implies that students don't learn at the same rate.

toring, cooperative learning, alternative assessments (including self-assessments), simulations, plays, projects, technology use, discussions, oral presentations, and team teaching.

5. Use energizers, such as name games, competitions with spelling words, and math contests.

6. Prepare students for an activity, have them complete the activity, and debrief them on the activity during the same block of time.

7. Teach time management by giving students multiple tasks/projects and letting them budget their time for completion.

8. Have students take turns keeping a daily log of activities, handouts, homework examples, and so on, in order to help those who are absent.

Adjusting to the Time Change

At first, teaching the longer blocks of time was very difficult and tiring. After having time to get used to it, though, the teaching has become easier. (See *Three Points of View* page 79) Yes, we are covering less material, so selective abandonment does need to take place. It does seem to be a much more humane atmosphere, however, as teachers work with fewer students each day.

Now, when we have a shortened period because of a half day, teaching for "only" 50 minutes seems rushed, and we have a hard time getting everything done.

The students have adapted very well to the new schedule. They say they like having fewer classes to focus on at one time and being able to finish a year-long class in 18 weeks. Students believe they have more choices now because they can take eight classes in a year

instead of seven. They also say they come to school more because it is more costly to miss a class. Their strongest criticism is that when a teacher is "boring," 90-minute classes can seem *very* long.

We did an informal survey in some classes a few weeks ago, and overwhelmingly, the students preferred to stay with the four-period day instead of returning to the old schedule.

Evaluating the Time Change

We attribute many successes to our four-period day. Here are some of the most significant ones:

• Having fewer students per day allows teachers to better monitor at-risk students.

• The longer blocks of time have allowed more

project learning to take place, especially in the lab courses.

• Attendance has improved; as the students say, "It is harder to skip a class now because we miss so much."

• Students' grades have improved, with fewer students failing.

• There is more time to use cooperative learning in the classroom.

• Both the students' and teachers' day is less fragmented and rushed because of fewer class changes.

Students have adapted well to the change. Along with the positive outcomes of the four-period day, some challenges have emerged:

• We are still trying to determine the best way to place transfer students.

• The outset was more tiring than we originally expected.

• We need to have a way to deal with students who are failing after nine weeks, so that they don't lose a whole course of credit.

• A lot of time has to go into scheduling each student.

• Planning for each period takes a lot of time on the teachers' part.

At this point, the successes outnumber the challenges, and overall, most people seem to be in favor of the change.

Recommendations For Potential Change Makers

For educators interested in restructuring their school schedule, we recommend the following:

• Make the transition for the right reason—to facilitate instruction.

• Work to improve assessment, and include it in instruction.

• Modify the curriculum to suit the new structure.

• Facilitate a shared decision-making model.

• Watch for the implementation dip. (There's a lot of trial and error involved in learning new ways!)

• Include students and parents in the planning

Our School:
North Eugene High School is one of four high schools in Eugene School District 4J in Oregon. It serves 1,100 students and maintains a stability index of 73 percent. Our Hispanic population is now at seven percent, followed by a four-percent African American population. Twelve and seven-tenths percent of our students are on the free or reduced-price lunch program. Our Advanced Placement enrollment is currently 44 percent.

Our City:
Eugene is the home of the University of Oregon, a major university that enrolls approximately 17,000 students. The city has diversified (through various types of small businesses) from its former focus of harvesting timber. Like most other cities in Oregon, Eugene is experiencing a change in demographics as our minority population is rapidly growing.

Our State:
Oregon, while on the leading edge of school restructuring with the passage of House Bill 3565 (which features Certificates of Initial Mastery and Advanced Mastery) is struggling with severe financial problems. A property tax limitation was passed two years ago, and a recent sales tax measure to help fund education was defeated by a large margin. In addition, an equalization law is now in effect that prohibits local communities from funding anything other than bond levies for maintenance of buildings and some capital outlays. Communities like Eugene that have good local support for education are being hit the hardest because excellent programs that require funding have been established and will now be difficult to maintain.

and decision-making process.

• Create an environment that encourages change and fosters the development of a shared vision.

• Conduct an assessment of staff needs before implementation.

• Understand that it takes time and resources to make the transition. ◆

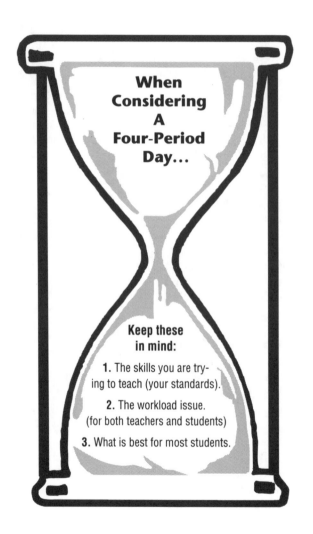

When Considering A Four-Period Day...

Keep these in mind:

1. The skills you are trying to teach (your standards).

2. The workload issue. (for both teachers and students)

3. What is best for most students.

Three Points of View

Following are our personal points of view on adjusting to the recent time change at Oregon's North Eugene High School.

Kevin McCauley
Biology Teacher

As a biology teacher, I viewed North Eugene High's decision to change to a four-period daily schedule in the 1993-94 school year with both interest and enthusiasm. In the traditional seven-period day, I was often frustrated by the limited time students had to complete a laboratory investigation or to work together on large-scale projects. Having 90 minutes instead of 50 to engage students in research tasks seemed a very positive development in North's restructuring process, and my colleagues in the science department shared my enthusiasm.

Piloting a two-period block class during the previous year gave me an opportunity to test the waters. I found that students were able to complete more labs in a single class, they worked more effectively on team projects, the classroom atmosphere was calmer and more conducive to learning, and I was able to give more individual attention to students because I had fewer students to interact with on a given day. Thus, my experience with a longer class period was sufficiently positive to induce me to dive in wholeheartedly.

I was a bit discomfited, therefore, this past fall when I encountered some unexpected difficulties as I adapted my life science curriculum to fit a four-period schedule. Because students complete a year-long course in 18 weeks, the question of whether sufficient content could be covered loomed in everyone's mind. What I've discovered is that I don't seem to cover as much material as I used to during a complete term; most students are limited in how much biological science they can learn in a single day. Difficult topics, such as cell respiration and protein synthesis, require several days to really be understood by a student. On the other hand, process skills, such as writing or working collaboratively, were enhanced by the 90-minute period. Student papers were more carefully written and had greater depth.

One of the papers I assigned my students was to explore the regionally important controversy surrounding the survival of the Pacific salmon species. Students were expected to develop a salmon management plan that would explore a number of competing interests. I assessed their plans by using a North-generated Writing Evaluation that I tailored to fit the assignment. Some students met the standard at an 80 percent or better level in the first try, while others rewrote the plans as many as four times. The students and I were struck by the fact that it wasn't "business as usual" in Biology. Many of my students were upset by having to do a number of rewrites, while I was frustrated by the time I spent coaching them through the task. However, the pride I saw displayed in the faces of my students when they met the standard more than compensated me.

As a result of restructuring, student work has more depth and is of higher quality. This has forced me into a process of "selective abandonment" in which I've had to determine what significant content needed to remain and what content should be let go to encourage process-skills development. The standards have helped shape what I teach, how I teach, and how I assess. The desired outcomes are beginning to drive the curriculum.

Julie Taylor
Foreign Language Teacher

The change process impacted Kevin, a biology teacher, differently than it impacted me, a foreign language teacher. In the beginning, neither I nor my department felt any need to change the structure of the day. We thought that our program was successful: our classes were always full to overfull, most students seemed to enjoy our classes, we were working in a student-centered learning environment, our AP program had a high success rate, and the students that went on to take a foreign language in college did very well.

As department chairperson, it was my task to learn more about the four-period day. Our reasons for being apprehensive included: How could we keep freshmen in a 90-minute block at the first-year level practicing the language for such an extended time when they knew so little? Would there be more discipline problems, especially with the freshman students? Because it takes time for a new language to sink in, how could we cover the same amount of material in one semester that we were used to doing in a year? What would the retention rate be if students went a semester or two without taking a language (i.e., say they take Spanish 1 first semester as freshmen and don't take Spanish 2 until the first or second semester as sophomores)?

The foreign language teachers in the schools I talked to were overwhelmingly supportive of the four-period day. We were told that the retention loss was not any greater for a nine-month lay-off than for a normal summer vacation. We were already used to doing a variety of activities (five to seven) in a 50-minute period, so we would need to create an even more student-centered classroom environment by using more cooperative learning strategies. It didn't appear that the same amount of material could be covered, but we recognized that learning could take place at a deeper level. After much discussion within the department, we agreed to support the implementation of the four-period day.

To ensure that sufficient content would be covered before the students took Advanced Placement (AP) exams, we changed our program from having the Advanced Placement class be the fourth course taken (AP was Spanish/French 4) to having it be the fifth course taken. What was previously taught in three year-long courses would now be taught in four 18-week-long blocks.

We knew that the change would be difficult—and it has been—but we felt that there would be enough advantages to make it worthwhile. In an informal survey of the department done a short time ago, we decided that if we had to choose to stay with the four-period day or to go back to the seven-period day, we would rather stay with our current schedule.

Bob Anderson
Principal

Kevin and Julie are two of our teacher leaders from different disciplines who are making time adjustments. The science teachers thought the transition would be relatively easy, while the foreign language and math teachers thought the transition would be difficult. We found that all staff members have experienced some level of difficulty, but have developed processes for overcoming these difficulties.

From a principal's viewpoint, the advantage we have had at North Eugene High lies in taking the time over the last seven years to make our restructuring a teacher-driven approach. I enjoy using a facilitative leadership approach. To observe the commitment level of the entire staff to innovation that better meets the needs of students is very rewarding. The time it has taken to move to a consensus model of decision making, to move from a teacher-directed classroom to a student-centered classroom, to make cooperative learning a productive aspect of learning, and to develop a broad-based leadership concept to be operational at North has been considerable; however, implementing top-down directives to put these concepts in place would have been a much more painful process.

The use of parents and students on committees along with faculty has been very valuable in moving the organization. Without their support and insight into the decision-making process, we would have made more mistakes.

Suggested Structures for 90-Minute Periods

MODEL A	MODEL B
1. Opening	1. Transition Activity (i.e., discuss current news, review past lesson)
2. Direct Instruction	2. Two or More Main Activities (i.e., reading, discussion, movie, small group work, simulation)
3. Breakout: Interactive/Cooperative Learning	3. Closure

Suggested Structures for 90-Minute Periods (continued)

MODEL C	MODEL D
1. Teacher Input	1. Opening
2. Student Grouping to Process the Input	2. Reading
3. Debriefing (i.e., How well did we work as a group?)	3. Discussion (i.e., What did you learn from the reading?)
4. Individual Accountability (last 30 or so minutes: quiz, homework, portfolio sample, self-assessment activity)	4. Work in Small Groups with Newly Acquired Information
	5. Closure

Reader Reflections

Insights: _____

_____

_____

_____

_____

Actions for Our School (District) to Consider: _____

_____

_____

_____

_____

_____

_____

Good schools are places where people learn from each other and care about each other.

Ernest Boyer
The Carnegie Foundation

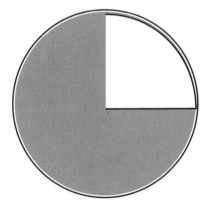

Short Stories

Following are brief accounts of how other schools across the country are restructuring school time. (Source: *NEA Today*.)

➤At Jackson Road Elementary School in Montgomery County, Maryland, approximately every two months, small groups of educators meet for four hours during the school day to discuss problems they encounter in their work with children.

Each group, called an *inquiry group*, consists of four or five classroom teachers, an education researcher from the local university, and an administrator or two. As a group, these educators discuss problems, pose and test solutions, and draw conclusions from the results.

Specially trained student teachers cover for classroom teachers when they attend inquiry group sessions.

➤At Ma'ili Elementary School on Oahu, Hawaii, 56 teachers spend up to an hour commuting to school each day—and another hour getting home. Until recently, these long commutes were causing as much as half of the school's staff members to leave as soon as they received tenure. To stop the teacher exodus, Ma'ili's school/community-based management team adopted a four-day week.

The academic schedule now runs Monday through Thursday. When the school was on a five-day week, Ma'ili classes started at 7:30 a.m. and ran until 2 p.m.

four days a week, and until 1:25 p.m. the fifth day. Today, classes start at 7:15 a.m. and run until 2:30 p.m. Recess and lunch periods have been shortened. Also, teachers have given back five days of professional development, which were formally conducted on Fridays.

On Fridays, Ma'ili offers students and all other community members optional enrichment courses, and teachers can instruct one of those courses for extra pay if they want. Only a handful do. But that doesn't mean that teachers don't spend their Fridays on school-related activities. Many use Friday as a planning day at home or at a resource center.

➤Members of the South Kinsap (Washington) Education Association purchased time by negotiating TRI— Time, Responsibility, and Incentive—grants of up to $2,000 a year. The grants pay for classes and conference fees, or for time spent on extracurricular supervision, planning, or rewriting curricula.

➤In Merrit Island, Florida, the Gardendale Elementary Magnet School has adopted a year-round calendar, with three-week intersessions between quarters. During these intersessions, teachers receive compensatory pay to meet for three or four days to work on curriculum planning.

➤Central Park East Secondary School in New York City

a combined junior and senior high school with 450 students. It is composed of three divisions, each with two houses—or two sets of students and teachers who work together. One morning a week, students within the same house engage in community service. On that morning, their teachers meet for group collaboration efforts until noon, when the students return to school.

Staff at Wells (Maine) Junior High School save time by reserving faculty meetings for substantive issues only. Faculty members use memos and bulletin boards to communicate all other information.

Classroom instruction begins one and a half hours later than usual on Wednesdays at Will C. Wood High School in Sacramento, California. Teachers use the one and a half hours for small-group planning sessions.

Every Wednesday at 2 p.m., all students in Ames, Iowa, schools are dismissed so that teachers can attend staff development sessions from 2:00 to 4:30 p.m.

Kapaa Elementary School, on Kauai, Hawaii, has opened six schools within a school to accommodate 1,500 students. The school structure is now large enough to maintain a supplemental staff of art, music, physical education, computer, speech-drama, and gifted specialists, who meet with various classes (rather than schedule classes of their own).

The principal has asked the supplemental staffers to collaborate on a half-day program, which they will present (as a team) successively in each of the six smaller schools. After rotating one program through all six schools, they will design another program.

➤Once every two weeks, staff at Susquehanna (Pennsylvania) Township Middle School get together before school starts to share ideas. The discussion moves into morning homeroom and lasts an additional 45 minutes. But that's OK, because on these meeting days, the principal leads a discussion among all students in the auditorium.

➤In order to create more time for faculty collaboration at Los Naranjos Elementary School in Irvine, California, teachers worked with parents to gain support for two time changes that would close the schools to student instruction and allow teachers to meet and plan.

The time changes were: (1) taking eight days out of students' school year and designating them as school improvement days and (2) dismissing students at 1 p.m. on Wednesdays.

Teachers convinced parents that if they wanted the improvements they were beginning to see to continue, they must give teachers time to work on them. During this outreach process, parents themselves chose to schedule the school improvement days immediately following holidays.

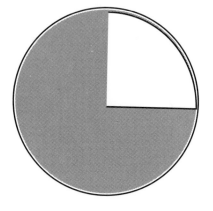

Selected Resources

Books

Anderson, L. W., ed. 1984. *Time and School Learning.* New York: St. Martin's Press.

Barrett, P.A., ed. 1991. *Doubts and Certainties: Working Together to Restructure Schools.* Washington, D.C.: National Education Association.

Carroll, J. M. 1989. *The Copernican Plan: Restructuring the American High School.* Andover, Mass.: The Regional Laboratory for Educational Improvement of the Northeast and Islands.

Covey, S. R. 1989. *The Seven Habits of Highly Effective People.* New York: Fireside.

Garfield, C. A. 1984. *Peak Performers.* New York: Avon.

Good, T. L. , and Brophy, J. E. 1991. *Looking in Classrooms.* New York: Harper and Row.

Jacokes, L. E. 1990. *Finding Planning Time for School Improvement Activities: A Manual.* Wyoming, Mich.: Wyoming Public Schools.

Maeroff, G. I. 1988. *The Empowerment of Teachers.* New York: Teachers College Press.

Powell, A., Farrar, E., and Cohen, D. 1985. *Shopping Mall High School: Winners and Losers in the Educational Marketplace.* Boston: Houghton Mifflin.

Purnell, S., and Hill, P. 1992. *Time for Reform.* Santa Monica, Calif.: Rand.

Senge, P. 1990. *The Fifth Discipline: The Art and Practice of the Learning Organization.* New York: Doubleday.

Sizer, T. R. 1992. *Horace's School: Redesigning the American High School.* Boston: Houghton Mifflin.

Weinstock, R. 1973. *The Greening of the High School.* Dayton, Ohio: Educational Facilities Laboratories.

Articles, Papers, Reports, and Documents

Baker, J., Bratigan, N., McElliot, K., and Withrow, J. 1990. "How Schools Create Time." Paper presented at the First International Symposium on Action Research, Vancouver, WA.

Bird, T., and Little, J.W. 1986. "How Schools Organize the Teaching Profession," *Elementary School Journal*, 86 (4) 493-511.

Brown, S. 1991. "The Role of Time in Teachers' Perceptions of their Own Teaching." Paper presented at the Annual Meeting of the American Educational Research Association, Chicago.

Canady, R. L., and Rettig, M. D. 1993. "Unlocking the Lockstep High School Schedule," *Phi Delta Kappan*, 75(4) 310-14.

Castle, S., and Watts, G. 1992. "The Tyranny of Time," *Doubts and Certainties* newsletter, 7(2) 1-4.

Center on Organization and Restructuring Schools. 1992. "Collaborative Planning Time for Teachers," Brief to Principals, No. 2, Madison, Wis.

Coalition of Essential Schools. 1991. "Resistant Teachers as a Force for Change," *Horace*, 7(3), 11-12.

Conley, D. T. 1993. "Roadmap to Restructuring," paper, Eric Clearinghouse on Educational Management.

Deming, W. E. 1981-82. "Improvement of Quality and Productivity Through Action by Management," *National Productivity Review*, 1 (Winter) 12-22.

Donahoe, T. 1993. "Finding the Way: Structure, Time, and Culture in School Improvement," *Phi Delta Kappan*, 75(4) 298-305.

Florida Commission on Education Reform and Accountability. 1991. "Blueprint 2000: The Florida Education Reform and Accountability Act." Tallahassee, Fla.

Handal, G. 1991. "Collective Time—Collective Practice?" Paper presented at the Annual Meeting of the American Educational Research Association, Chicago.

Hargreaves, A. 1990. "Teachers' Work and the Politics of Time and Space," *Qualitative Studies in Education*, 3(4) 303-20.

Keyes, R. 1992. "Do You Have Time?" *Parade Magazine*, February 16, pp. 22-25.

Little, J. W. 1984. "Norms of Collegiality and Experimentation: Conditions for School Success," *American Education Research Journal*, 19, 325-40.

Louis, K. S., and Smith, B. 1990. "Teachers' Work: Current Issues and Prospects for Reform." In P. Reyes (ed.), *Productivity and Performance in Educational Organizations*. Newbury Park, Calif.: Sage.

Prager, K. 1992. "Collaborative Planning Time for Teachers," Brief to Principals, No. 2. Center on Organization and Restructuring of Schools.

Price, H. B. 1993. "Teacher Professional Development It's About Time," *Education Week*, May 12, pp. 24, 32.

Ringle, P. M. , and Savickas, M. L. 1983. "Administrative Leadership: Planning and Time Perspectives," *Journal of Higher Education*, 54(6): 649-61.

Sommerfeld, M. 1993. "Time and Space," *Education Week*, March 13, pp. 13-19.

Spady, W. G. 1992. "It's Time to Take a Close Look at Outcome-Based Education,"*Outcomes*, Summer, pp. 6-13.

Vatts, G., and Castle, S. 1993. "The Time Dilemma in chool Restructuring," *Phi Delta Kappan*, 75(4) 306-09.

Villis, S. 1993. "Are Longer Classes Better?" *Update* ewsletter, 35(3) March. Washington, D.C.: Association or Supervision and Curriculum Development.

Notes:

_____

_____

_____

_____

_____

_____

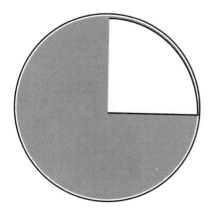

Glossary

Better-Used Time
Using currently scheduled meetings and professional development activities more effectively by focusing on planning and collaboration.

Block Scheduling
Restructuring the school day into fewer, longer instructional time blocks. For example, a typical daily high school divides its instructional time into seven 50-minute periods. If it were to use block scheduling, it might divide the instructional day into four 90-minute periods.

Common Time
Time designated for teacher collaboration and the development of "facultyness." During such time, colleagues with similar assignments work together on restructuring programs, interdisciplinary teams, subject-area collaboration, and/or grade-level planning.

Early Release Day
Day on which a school operates a shortened schedule and students go home a few hours early. After the students leave, the school staff meets to work in areas such as school improvement.

Freed-Up Time
Using various arrangements to free teachers from direct student supervision. These include enlisting administrators to teach classes, authorizing teaching assistants and college interns to teach classes at regular intervals under the direction of a teacher, and teaming teachers in a way that allows one teacher to instruct for another.

Professional Education (ProEd) Day
Workday set aside for districtwide workshops or traditional end-of-semester planning.

Purchased Time
Hiring additional teachers, clerks, parents, and support staff to allow for smaller class sizes and/or expanded or additional planning sessions.

Restructured Time
Formally altering the time frame of the traditional school calendar, school day, or teaching schedule.

Timelock
The feeling that demands on our time become so overwhelming that we cannot wring one more second out of crowded schedules and hectic days.

Temporary Duty Elsewhere (TDE) Day
Day on which official permission is granted for a school staff member to be out of his or her regular work site and still on the district payroll. The staff member does not have to use sick leave or personal time, is covered by Workman's Compensation, and is provided with a substitute.

Reform cannot be carried out during teachers' spare time.
If reform is to be effective, the job description
of the teacher has to change.

Gene Maeroff
The Empowerment of Teachers

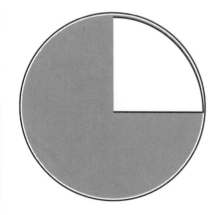